EMOTIONS OF RETIREMENT

*The Anguish of Leaving
Your Business Behind*

ROSE CATALANO

Emotions of Retirement
Copyright © 2021 by Rose Catalano

All rights reserved. No part of this publication may be reproduced, distributed, or transmitted in any form or by any means, including photocopying, recording, or other electronic or mechanical methods, without the prior written permission of the author, except in the case of brief quotations embodied in critical reviews and certain other non-commercial uses permitted by copyright law.

The views expressed in this work are solely those of the author and do not necessarily reflect the views of the publisher, and the publisher hereby disclaims any responsibility for them.

ISBN
978-1-954932-82-1 (Paperback)
978-1-954932-81-4 (eBook)

CONTENTS

Acknowledgements vii
Preface xiii

Emotions of Retirement 1
New Bursary Perception 27
Time Is Of The Essence 37
Mixed Emotions 45
The Quest For Serenity 57
The Boomers' Way 65
The Financial GPS 83
When Is The Right Time? 97
Technology Is To Blame 111
The Alternatives 123
The Exit Plan And The Reward 133
Slowing Down 165
The Groundwork Days 183

About the Author 191

ACKNOWLEDGEMENTS

Thank you to all the baby boomers and recent retirees who willingly shared their stories of past decades. Thank you for your foresight and courage to bring change to the communities at large. Your strength of mind opened the doors to progress that have positively impacted many people for many years.

To my daughter Sabina and my son David,
May good fortune be your life-long companion,
May your days bring you endless smiles,
and may all your wishes come true.

                                        Love always

                                        mom/re

Also by Rose Catalano

This Head of Security Wears High Heels

A Child's Voyage to New Life

Available through Amazon.com

PREFACE

Today we live in a fast-paced world overwhelmed by technology. How can middle-aged people steer toward a goal of minimalism while moving closer to their golden days?

Even with acquired acumen and an accumulated series of proceedings, it is still a challenge for baby boomers or anyone else considering departure from their work environment to an uncomplicated semi- retirement or a fully retired lifestyle.

The first wave of boomers has entered retirement, and we stand to learn a lot from them. Their experience explains whether they were fearful and even a little apprehensive about the benefits of work withdrawal, or whether they counted down the days to giving up work. If we look closely, we can often detect an unchecked look of confusion on some retirees' faces as they realize the rapidity in which days and years have slipped by unnoticed.

Living in any form of confusion, or feeling that we're trekking alone in the rotation of life is not a good place to be, but, once in a while, a little confusion can push us to pay enough attention to our surroundings so that life actually begins to make sense.

Ageing is a fragile development. The ability to accept the phenomenon gracefully gives us the authority to become enlightened adults. By the time we become adults, we have reached the age of maturity and have developed characteristics that demonstrate an established outlook in life. As we commence our journey toward this stage of our lives, we should be able to distinguish real issues from trivialities. The reality of retirement age does not approach us as an outstanding issue waiting to be resolved nor does it represent a triviality. It is merely a fact!

Days form the unbroken passage of time throughout our existence as we move through successive occasions from beginning to end.

Education, scientific advancements, sports, medical research, entrepreneurship and other diverse occupational fields all incorporate the notion of time into their project evaluations.

As grownups, we become more and more aware of the importance of time and of a person's lifespan. Thus, the prospect of approaching retirement age is no longer an elective for us.

Some of us may find planning for the impending retirement an exhilarating experience, while others may declare it a discretionary activity.

Whether we choose to make retirement plans as we go along or prefer to plan in advance, it is important to have a clear vision of how we want to spend our days once work is gone. It really is up to us to figure out how we can live retired life to its fullest.

"The unexamined life is not worth living." - Socrates

EMOTIONS OF RETIREMENT

In the early morning of February 24, 2016, I awoke to the incessant reverberation of the house phone. The persistent individual trying to contact me was my younger brother, Mike, wanting to make sure he was the first to extend his best wishes for my birthday.

As in past years, the day was outdone by the number of additional calls received from new acquaintances combined with my long time-well-wishers who have never missed a birthday greeting.

Although the conversational exchanges were kept short and contained a methodical pattern, all pleasantries ended with that same inescapably rhetorical question: *"OK, are you ready for early retirement now?"*

Was I to classify this as a dismissive question or address it with disarming openness? I had so much more work to do and so many projects on the go that the thought of slowing down had not occurred to me. The recipe for my up-and-coming business strategy did not include the gamut of sentiments that suggested switching from the speedy lane to motoring along a more relaxed pace. Until now, descending to the lower physics of energy had been neither earmarked nor highlighted in my daily planner.

The closest I had come to retirement was listening to several jokes about the elderly while in the company of a mixed age group, or in a restaurant, where the word "senior" came with a 15 percent discount.

As far as I was concerned, retirement was my parents' territory. I didn't belong there yet. Why could these people not see that? Was it because I had put on a few unwanted pounds and my waistline looked a little inflated? Was there something odd about the way I walked or spoke?

Maybe it was the fact that I didn't wear stiletto heels. My foot wear of preference and comfort had switched from high heels to flat shoes that slipped on and off with ease.

Those unpleasant retirement questions made me feel so flustered I was unable to think or focus on anything else. How could this be happening to me? I'm still the woman capable of making quick and rational decisions, solving problems speedily, keeping a good steady pace all day long, and functioning with only a few hours of sleep when necessary.

But, for some reason, today, the persistent question gnawed at my heart, although for the most part, my feelings were not considered extra sensitive or fragile. So how did the simple questions of early retirement leave me in such a confused state? Could it be possible that the so called "golden years" were quietly making a mark on my calendar? If so, my faithful planner had become a dishonest friend intent on deceiving my delicate feelings. Then again, the truth was obvious: The years had been creeping up on me while I believed I was indomitable. With that thought creating a heavy atmosphere, my smile was washed off my face. I felt tongue-tied.

Did I have a secret confession to make? To whom could I confess my age phobia? Maybe my mother would be a good confessor --- but would she still have the presence of mind to come up with a quick and frank absolution for me. I felt sure if I confided in my mother, my dilemma would be kept private. That assumption provided some relief since for a few years now, I had become aware that any time I shared a secret with my mother, a senior citizen aged eighty-five plus, the story remained safe. There was also a first-rate chance my mother would not remember the story anyway. If she did remember the conversation and wanted to share it with other family members or neighbours, there was a strong probability she could not recall details accurately. If she were told, her modified version may simply come across more like a personal opinion rather than a repeat of a private conversation.

It is an undeniable fact that ageing along with facing daily growth and development, is inevitable.

Granted, after sixty-some years of existence, I should have had a good grasp of this verdict. Instead, it was hard for me to believe I would be on a more advantageous plateau had I remedied my thoughts and placed myself in harmony with the inescapable aging progress. After all, isn't going through the full cycle of life with the expectation of living to a ripe old age like a pilgrimage of anticipation?

In the past, I always managed to keep a relatively cool attitude when in the company of senior citizens, and have spent many enjoyable hours with people living their twilight years. Of special interest are those afflicted with the negative physical or mental effects of old age. It hasn't been unusual for me to engage in discussions regarding their health or energy limitations. On many occasions I have been a witness to identity detachment while observing the cumbersome movements of senior citizens who have lost their hopes and ambitions. But here is the surprising part: I constantly keep myself active by reading and learning as much as I can in relation to such conditions. As a result, I feel confident enough to offer reasonable support or an alternate option to assist burdened seniors deal with various hindrances.

In my ongoing mission to help, I've learned a very important lesson from the retirees who have mastered the art of brushing off the more menial stressors of their daily lives. They have taught me that a delightful life is most likely to be found by allowing happiness to act as an inside regulator. This, in turn, promotes longevity, a greater sense of purpose, and a measure of overall well being. This blueprint has brought many seniors renewed authenticity.

Am I to consider this as merely the initial fear facing mature adults as we try to accept what scares us into admitting we're no longer young? Does approaching retirement age suggest people no longer look attractive or feel full of energy? Do we, as mature adults, fear that our jobs make us feel less valued or not really needed? Does everyone really look and judge the ageing population from the exterior only? After a few hours had passed without finding any answers to my questions, I turned my thoughts back to my mother with whom I spend a substantial amount of time. I usually set aside several hours each week, ensuring my mother, a senior with a big heart and diminishing strength, is not missing out on anything. I make certain her personal appointments are kept up-to-date, and that the housekeeper continues to provide good service for her.

As my thoughts focused on past occasions when the family gathered for birthday celebrations and other significant festivities. I noticed that my mother smiled a lot but was not particularly conversant. In fact, she didn't partake in many conversations nor did she initiate new dialogues. Months later, I realized she was hard of hearing and to cover it up, she simply smiled pretending she was in the know. Was this a virtue or a vice?

I switched my attention to the time my father turned his ripe retirement age of sixty-five and I could still recall how positive he had been about the benefits of retirement. He always said that with an adequate income and a positive attitude, the elderly of his era had every opportunity to live a splendid life. His favourite pastime was his passion for telling jokes. He enjoyed good meals, appreciated the taste of excellent wines, loved our family without reservation and definitely valued his time congregating at the local bar with other members of the community. He loved to watch the younger generation struggle to find their way in the world, and coyly remarked at the number of tattoos each person had decorated themselves with. He saw this phenomenon as a cultural loneliness and believed that in thirty or forty years, these tattooed people would look rather peculiar when their skin started to wrinkle. I don't think he ever really understood the psychology behind the tattoo revolution. But as he grew older, and closer to his eighties and nineties, his perception of retirement slowly but consistently changed. What he once found to be fabulous days of retirement now were addressed as days of hardship. The pension benefits he had previously deemed quite sufficient, now were finances to be monitored carefully. Whereas once he took pleasure in spending time at the bar, he now no longer spent time to visit that same block. Nevertheless, one thing that remained intact was his ability to tell jokes and poke fun at any given situation. One of the bar jokes that remained embedded in my mind was the story of an elderly gentleman slowly making his way to a dessert bar. An old man anxiously makes his way into the bar and although he limps and trembles, he eventually manages to climb up and sit on a stool. The bartender noticed he was having difficulties moving around and asked if there was something he could get for him. The old man says he would like a glass of water and a banana split. "Crushed nuts?" the bartender asks. The old man sadly responds "no, it's arthritis."

Those are among the personal moments we cherished and shared as a family. I pocketed many belly aching laughs from those happy occasions. Still, I'm not prepared to admit to myself or to my friends and family that my retirement juncture is only a short distance away. This reluctance holds especially true today in view of it being another one of my over the sixty birthdays. In my eyes, this occasion marks another short mile travelled toward my life's stretch. What is all this absurdity my cohorts dole out so freely? This day hardly feels like the right time to let bewilderment force my happy event into a place assigned to mature audiences only. When I woke up in the morning, I had no idea this particular birthday would turn into a gala in reverence to life's *tour de force*. Now, just a few hours into the day, I can almost hear my heart starting to beat like a cat's heart, measuring somewhere between 160 and 200 beats per minute. This was not a comforting predicament to be in, but I managed to keep going without the need of an oxygen mask or a defibrillator.

By nature, I tend to be a resilient individual who marches through life accepting and overcoming whatever pains may accompany personal growth. I strive to keep myself in the present, and I most certainly believe in tomorrow. It would not be incorrect to say I'm determined to stay the course when many others would find themselves in the throes of dread and gloom should circumstances hit a negative state. Today, however, I was being asked to concede that I had a muted but prevailing weak point. I was ignoring the responsibility to consider retiring from my company.

I have worked hard to build a successful business, raise my two children with all the care, love, and guidance I could master and, in the process; I never showed signs of slowing down or suffering from fatigue.

Today, I still believe that most of my ideas are considered innovative and well thought-out with respect to my occupation and family endeavors. I keep up with the day-to-day operation of the business, although from time to time I entertain the prospect of taking it down a notch or two. I get tickled by the likelihood of having more occasions to unwind and socialize with friends and family. I look forward to the opportunity of having more time to lend a hand to the not-for-profit foundation I so eagerly support. There is also another conscious strategy of great importance to me: the chance to enjoy precious time with my grandson, Dillon. Admittedly, I'm guilty of not leaning toward making any of these adjustments today or in the immediate future, but I do understand that if I continue procrastinating day after day and year after year, nothing will change. Things might actually start getting worse as I grow older and my stamina becomes weaker. I do realize that without making life style corrections, I could risk missing out on a lot.

In my middle-age, the truth is that I continue to work long days, fighting account collection battles side by side with my administrative staff, and playing devil's advocate with my sales team. In no way I feel I have outgrown my business or that the business has outgrown me. When at the office, I make sure I stand tall and visible and remain balanced throughout nonstop operational demands. At times, I'm so deep in thought about business activities that I must surely look like a permanent fixture or a full length portrait. Experience has taught me never to claim myself as a supreme champion of anything, but I can definitely carry myself as a solid business defender.

Sighing frequently, if ever so softly, I allow my head to inflate with half measures of strength as I think of the occasional, fairly good-natured teasing remarks I received from friends and family in the morning. As far as I can determine, they innocently have missed my barometric mark. Consequently, I experience bizarre bouts of contentious thoughts and feelings. Not many favourable results can be drawn from their well-meant words, nor do the first hours of the day turn out to be pleasant or useful for me. At this point, I feel startled and have had enough of everyone.

Could it be that the good wishes *du jour* were delivered with a concealed riddle for the birthday girl to unravel? Even so, I was not ready or willing to consider this as a contented exchange, and besides, why must life have to have labels anyways?

With some measure of graciousness, they all had intentionally, or perhaps inadvertently, unleashed a tsunami of questions about my continuation in the work force. Their actions, however, had only managed to dole out loads of deflated ego. There was nothing subtle about that. I may not be sitting at the helm of my youth, but, I'm not over the hill either. Thus far, the day hasn't done much to boost my self-assurance. Nonetheless, I didn't crumble under their disquieting grilling.

Slowly but surely, I did try to categorize the dynamics of growing older and would agree that one cannot and should not conveniently, or falsely, work against the ageing process. On the other hand, I'm not prepared to let this odd feeling linger, nor do I want to perceive this day as the appropriate occasion for winding down. I came to this conclusion because I still feel abundantly vibrant. I carry my age well, feel reasonably healthy, am repeatedly told I look younger than my years and am still capable of making decisions on the spot. Yet, I had a sneaky suspicion that at some point in the next few days/months/years, all this would change, and I would face some rigid lessons ahead.

Inwardly, I feel the stakes are growing a little higher for me. At my age, I fear I might become more vulnerable to some serious health issues that could cause me to make a bad business decision and consequently turn into a costly error resulting in a slim financial bottom line.

I told myself that, as people, we are an imperfect bunch and are therefore subject to making mistakes even when trying hard and feeling our best. Living up to our perfect ideals may well score lower than living with the ability to accept grey areas and stimulate the elasticity that allows us to make concessions. Perhaps this is the medicine a qualified therapist should recommend for me and for other undecided individuals wedged in the same pre-retirement space I find myself in. I've come to understand myself and my more sensitive tips. After a small display of defiance, I composed myself, set aside whatever emotional sentiment had crept into my mind throughout the morning, and determined that all those inquiries remained beside the point. This was not a day to be consumed by a blizzard of questions referencing the probability of my early retirement. All I wanted on this day was to savour every moment of a quiet time at home. But the intention of weaving my own yarn after repeated emphasis on my retirement status would not be realized.

What I fretted about most was dealing with the possibility of my infringing on the limits of human courtesy although none were being imposed on me. I confess that such an attitude was not befitting me, but my inaudible manners told me I had nothing to say about it. Typically, I prefer to take a common- sense approach to things, but because this occasion had surfaced bearing many startling twists and turns, I temporarily lost my mojo. Fueled by past experience, I reminded myself that some matters tend to carry more urgency and importance than others. With that in mind, I activated my re-tune button and redirected my focus back to my household principles and the significance of birthdays, life, and making a living.

By adopting clear-cut means of handling my approach, I abandoned my annoyances and verbalized each of those occasions to myself. I then continued on to reframe their meaning with my personal definitions. As we know, definitions can be thought-provoking on any given day and so, on this day; it became especially meaningful for me to develop my personal view of each occurrence.

Birthday:

- A time to celebrate one's day of birth.
- Another opportunity to figure out our existence.
- A day to recognize the accumulation of celebratory occasions.
- An opportunity to remind ourselves that getting older beats the alternative.
- A triumphant time to rejoice in our ability to outlive our rivals.

Life:

- Physically active beings that enjoy being animated versus those who choose to go through life without creative development or enthusiasm to form any intuitive influences.
- Getting a grip on the different stage of living: *First as a baby* – coddling, loving and playing. *Secondly, as a child* – believing we are invincible. *Thirdly, as a teenager* – we know everything. *Fourthly, as an adult* – getting a taste of reality; work, raising a family, proper nutrition, the value of exercise, and saving for retirement.

Mid-life – a crisis waiting to happen as we now see the world for what it really is.

Senior years – a chance to do things we had no time to do before. The opportunity to say we have been successful at living a long life then waste a lot of time complaining about all the aches and pains.

Making a living:

- Work to financially support yourself and/or your family
- Going to work as a means of making a living not living so that you can go to work.
- Getting up and going to work to avoid boredom or isolation by idling at home.
- An attitude and way of life that is dissimilar to the one practiced by swindlers and charlatans.

History has indeed shown us that work has the capacity to provide physical and mental stimulation among other benefits. In work, we can find the remedy to cure loneliness, overcome melancholic days, learn the synergy of team effort, acquire people skills, and, at times, even participate in social reform. With sufficient practice, even the most agitated or the shyest of people may dare to scrap their uncertainty and cash-in on the opportunity to conquer the fear of looking their superiors in the eyes when a business or personal discourse is taking place. Work could be referred to as the hub of the collective approach to life.

Indira Gandhi said: "There are two types of people, those who do the work and those who take the credit. Try to be in the first group, there is less competition there."

I don't believe it is purely perception that we live to tell our tale from a fundamentally ideological perspective or in a gloomy, unapologetic manner. As a rule, I've always chosen to live and work with a purpose; therefore, I believe I qualify as a fan of the first philosophy - "the excited principles." Granted, this may seem to be a strange, dubious, and despondent approach for those who detest the efforts of a good day's work. It goes without saying that if you have a habit of wanting more out of life but choose to do less; you will find yourself in a big mess. It is therefore advisable to engage in work and capitalize on the ingredient that gets us the essentials to satisfy our existence. How else can we enrich our lives and be a part of the locomotive that moves the economy forward? Through work, we are able to feed, house, and clothe ourselves. Work also often gives us the opportunity to develop a side piggybank that affords us a little travel and fun time. Employment, if and when selected and performed in good taste and with our best efforts, tends to be the component that adds to our lifestyle. In that case, work cannot merely be labeled as a daily exercise that gets us our paycheck. Some, if not most us, look at the commitment to work as a means of utilizing our knowledge and a way to strengthen our abilities in order to achieve a sense of personal enjoyment, economic participation and fulfillment. Others may find employment to be an unrewarding work-out and frequently get to feeling sick each time they are called to go to work. With that approach, there's a good chance, by the day's end, that these individuals will become exhausted and emotionally overdone. I find this brand of emotion and nonchalant behavior toward one's employment disconcerting but not at all new.

In direct contrast to that depiction, we all know someone who comes alive when at work and definitely thrives on those adrenaline binges. Their fondness for high-quality results remains unchanged even after they've put in too many personal hours. They experience irritability only when they don't know when to unplug. These highly committed individuals are routinely the first to arrive to work and the last to leave. They interpret a shorter work day as a slippery slope that can only lead to job insecurity. Contrary to popular belief, they do not consider the shortened working hours as an open invitation to scurry to the boss's office for some kind of employment clarification or status reassurance. Their only objective is to perform their assigned tasks with integrity and strive to achieve the pre-set goals with professionalism and self-fulfillment. I often refer to the individual with this personal characteristic as "the one who's going the distance in life."

It is natural and most gratifying to be pleased with employees who avoid unnecessary office drama and are gainfully occupied to stay at the cusp of the breaking business edge. Overall, I would say that if an employee has the skill to be a good judge of their time and responsibility, they should name their own time to disengage, decide when to let go from work, and when to turn their attention to their personal life. If we select properly, this delicate equilibrium of work and personal space is capable of delivering a well-balanced and productive life style. On those terms, we would be looking at a manner of living in which work could be described as the symbol of hope that facilitates self- development, personal achievement, and social skills.

We do a lot of learning at college or university, but the true test comes through hands-on experience even if education provides us with an endorsement that says we are trained and ready to do good work. Perhaps it's hard to believe but nevertheless fascinating to witness how the industrialized world is home to many people who love the work they do regardless of it being a low paying job. They are eager to rise early every morning to make a valuable contribution to their company and to society in general. They are of the conviction that this is what they do for a living and not what they *have* to do to live. They do not see their job as the kind of work that takes them nowhere; nor do they define it as a dead-end life.

Theodore Roosevelt, or known as the "Rough Rider" said it best in a speech of September 1902. "I don't pity any man who does hard work worth doing. I admire him. I pity the creature who does not work at whichever end of the social scale he may regard himself as being." Here stood a man who eloquently delivered a profound life meaning through his unmatched charisma and did it all without a shift in his resolve. He endorsed his commitment for reform in the workplace and modified governmental regulations for the industrial world and for consumer protection. He believed that hard work, dedication and ambitions are the most valuable attributes, and when administered well, serve to help all classes of citizens. Some will disavow the meaning of his words and find his message nothing more than irritating. Conversely, I've never found any reason to disagree with the significance of his words nor do I find an open edge in which to slot the slightest misinterpretation of his point. The meaning of his words was profound, real, and invigorating. In my estimation, his reference to the value of a "*man*" doing hard work conveyed a feeling of one's self-fulfillment, respect and gratitude. I do, however, recognize those days when political correctness did not include recognition of equality in their dialogue. In the present day, one can draw a parity appropriate and equally meaningful to gender, race, and religion.

On the flip side, for some individuals, the mere notion or commitment to work can sometime sound like a panic button. When not silenced in a timely manner, it can set off a voice-activated alarm that says "I don't care how you feel right now, get up, get dressed, and show up to work on time." Claiming to feel sluggish does not make your day any better and the only person in charge of your elation is you. Then there are those who wish for a labour magician to instantly appear and rescue them from the rut they got themselves into at work. These same individuals are inclined to prefer to sit back and yearn about winning the biggest lottery prize available so they can leave their employment and live happily ever after. They certainly have the prerogative to choose not to live a very productive life and may prefer wasting their days dreaming for riches at inopportune times or even in the wrong life spell. They may wish to fanaticize about cashing in their inheritance as an alternative to going to work. Is it even conceivable that their type of discontent can turn financial waves for them? Sadly, such daydreams and wishful thinking produce an unrealistic picture that elevates their dissatisfaction to an imagined superior plateau. For them, the thought of stretching far to reach for a distant piece of pie in the sky, is of equal to receiving an unwelcome invitation that bids them to participate in a "face the reality" symposium.

Sometimes, I can only scratch my head in disbelief when I inadvertently stumble upon a downbeat gloominess brought on by people who think the biggest advantage of team work is the opportunity to blame others for their mistakes. Another hilarity is knowing that some of my employees frequently accuse upper and middle management of being stupid. What they fail to realize is that management does not sit on a swivel chair all day long craving the hours away. Nor do they comprehend that management has neither the luxury nor flexibility to shut-off their cell phone, open their office door, and wait for the profits to come in. These dismal operators would quickly be out of a job if their counter-productive work ethics missed the mark and management decided not to excuse them. Instead, they are allowed to keep collecting an income while the upper team keeps investing more time and more money to retrain them in an attempt to correct their deficiencies.

I'm also well acquainted with the work ethics of people who accept menial assignments only to let their brain get some extra sleep. On occasion, I've had the questioning pleasure of dealing with employees who possess a jagged attitude. In the event a supervisor dares say anything to them, whether about a potential task or otherwise, their immediate response is a disturbing eye- rolling exercise. Might there be any sign of enthusiasm for their job sprouting from that horizon at any time in this century? Hustle and bustle are not implied as strong attributes in their short curriculum vitae (CV), but work, as a means of recreational time, certainly is. I'm hard pressed to see this process as a good pay-off, but I'm prepared to identify it as a prime example of people without goodwill freely running amok in our economy by dodging the bullets of responsibility. However, the working class is made up of a diverse faction of citizens, and one can always find a contrast of attitudes spread throughout society.

If we look hard enough, we may discover a unique approach to life. I refer to all that can be achieved wherever our domicile or whatever our current situation. Without attacking or categorizing anyone's employment views, or taking measure of the output from any group, I'm thankful for individuals who are not afraid to put in a good day's work, have no qualms about a forty hour work week, and who, at times, volunteer to remain on the job extra hours if their help is needed to meet the forecasted quota. These are the individuals I can easily relate to and with whom I celebrate both business victories and hard times.

Recently though, my daily energy levels for doing business battles are beginning to display a hint of sluggishness. The least amount of evidence that a variance could spitefully sneak up and upset the fold causes me to worry. The thought that my team might encounter an unforeseen pile of distractions as they plough through a busy work day leaves me agitated. At times, I lose sleep because of my concerns over what type of variable results a difficult business situation may produce. Will the end result justify the means? Will the challenge upset the fold and cause my management staff to lose their momentum for achieving in great volumes? Similar to many other business owners, I readily confess that I prefer not to make friends or enemies with words beginning with the letter "F" for fret, fatigue, or failure. I'd rather not have these words used as part of my organization's vocabulary. The desire to stay ahead of failure gives us the push to achieve positive results.

On a couple of occasions, I went as far as asking my two senior assistants to ensure they continue to work as if they were on a rescue mission. And if they detected that I was shying away from taking the lead, they were to pounce immediately on the opportunity to tell me to smarten up. This straightforward request worked like a whispered proposition that the time to start skirting tumultuous work days was getting close to my mark.

How do I decide on how much longer I should work? What bench-mark do I use to determine when I need a change of pace? Better still, when should I initiate a walk toward the exit sign that leads me to a place far away from the work force? Similar to other mature adults who are facing this test of time, I now came up against a lot of tough questions that draw different conclusions for each of us. When challenges come into view as hard topics to resolve and solid answers are slow in coming, I tend to do a lot of thinking and soul searching. Today was one of those days. I feel riddled with intrigue because my present retirement ordeal contains so many strange but fascinating qualities. I was not compelled to come up with an immediate retirement decision, but my heart knew I should pay heed to the reality before me.

At this point, I decided to switch from this line of thought and spice things up a bit. Why did I get into the service business in the first place? I even played with the idea of figuring out which nations are known to have the most service- oriented industries and which have the most dedicated labouring citizens. I admit, I've been a little naïve and unaware of the volume of such an undertaking, but being a stubborn woman, I wanted to know more about how the industrial world really functions. To accomplish that, I was prepared to go extraordinary lengths to learn as much as I could. I was especially intrigued by the similarities as well as the unusual cosmopolitan ethics of the world's working class.

A genuine buzz engulfed me once I plunged into a project study that disclosed the following particulars about the top ten nations known to work the hardest:

#1 Mexico

> Due to lower education levels, Mexicans work an average of approximately 1,800 hours a year or 10 hours per day. A substantial number of these citizens do good, steady work for the American southern border or for people of more advanced economies.

> Mexico is the 14th largest economy in the world today, but it has the 2nd highest level of income inequality and a high level of poverty. The average

household income is approximately $13,000 US per year.

#2 Japan

Japanese have legendary work ethics. Their workday consists of 12 hours or more, working beyond a 40-hour-a-week contract. Often, the first 20 hours of overtime are unpaid. Their devotion to the company that employs them demands total loyalty. A job for life means lifelong employment with one company.

#3 Portugal

Portuguese people work between 8 and 9 hours per day. Men work approximately 2 hours of unpaid labour each day. There is no "siesta time" allowed in their work day.

#4 Canada

A Canadian's work day comprises of approximately 7.5 hours to 8.5 hours per day. According to the Organization for Economic Cooperation and Development, we have the highest population of a foreign born work force and the second-highest level, after Iceland, of "positive experience," or employees feeling they are treated with respect. However, Canada ranks above average with employees complaining of pains, anxieties, gloom, pressure and depression.

#5 Estonia

Home to hard-working, reliable, and groundbreaking people who on average, work about 8.5 hours per day. They value their education system, and engage in their career while studying for their degree. Estonians will partake in volunteer work even after a long day's exertion. They do the highest unpaid work after Turkey, Mexico and Australia.

#6 Austria

Austrians work an average of 8.5 hours per day. They have one of the highest totals of paid and unpaid work hours. The nation has one of the lowest unemployment rates and lower income inequality.

There is no nationwide minimum wage standard, but they have industry-specific guidelines to abide by. It is reported that migrant workers face discrimination, and work in poor conditions.

#7 China

The Chinese work environment is highly structured and citizens work an average of 9.5 hours to 12 hours per day. They perform approximately 40 to 50 hours of unpaid overtime per month. People often work in unsafe conditions and training is scarce. Factory workers do piece-work and are never sure they will receive full payment.

#8 New Zealand

Employees work just over 8 hours per day or 40 hours per week.

They practice quality work/life balance. Even non-union members can take advantage of the collective agreement and use it as a basis for their employment conditions.

#9 United States of America

Americans work an average of 8 to 9 hours per day.

The average household income after taxes is approximately $31,000.

Pay inequality is an on-going subject for discussion and revision.

It is believed that only 30 to 35 percent of the workers feel their jobs lead to advancement. Many work at steady, predictable, and unexciting jobs.

About half the industrial workers report they face unpleasant and sometimes hazardous conditions.

#10 Slovak Republic

Because of high unemployment and lack of job security, Slovaks work exceptionally hard and put in long hours when the work is available. On average, a Slovak works a minimum of 3.5 hours of unpaid work per week.

Most companies hire contract workers from employment agencies for the purpose of maintaining the upper hand on wage control and the right to dismiss workers without notice.

When I started this research, it was difficult to encourage myself to see the commitment through since it demanded a degree of time I'm frequently short of. But, I felt that any new and meaningful information I might draw from this undertaking would unquestionably refine my knowledge.

NEW BURSARY PERCEPTION

From my research, I learned there is one common denominator that stands out with similar concerns in all industrialized and developing countries. I refer to the fear that retirement may not provide the assurance that we will not face a life-altering experience when work is no longer an option. The population is aging rapidly, and people are living much longer thanks to the benefits of medicine. The present retirement income format may be forced to change in the years to come because governments are in danger of facing a shortfall in their treasuries.

In the foreseeable future, there is a strong possibility we will be introduced to changes that may decrease the amount of entitled pension benefits.

It is conceivable that governing authorities will find it necessary to increase the age of early retirement, or perhaps devise more attractive incentives to promote private savings.

With the current rate of departure from the labour force, every citizen should venture into a well-planned agenda to uncover their ideal retirement income. Making it happen would be considered one of the most normal possessions of the ageing lore and would cement the unwritten claim of being transformative. This priority may prove to be hard to package, but it has the potential to produce somber economic implications. We must follow this matter through via reasonable research to determine what, if any, tax-exempt accounts are available to us as part of a prosperous portfolio. Notably, we should be in-the-know about current difficult social and economic predicaments that could plague the nation in the near future.

In my opinion, it is our responsibility to keep the well of social and financial positivity firmly within our grasp. However, this may be difficult if we remain averse to conflict.

By putting irritability aside, we're able to keep a clear head for which to examine what's best for ourselves. I believed that being educated about potential tax exemptions and other financial benefits is one of the best provisos for the journey to a successful retirement.

I do my best to keep up-to-date on this subject by sifting through various options with the potential to endorse my plans, and I shun away from risks that conceivably could assault my financial stability. Overall, I'm open to taking a chance on the hope there really will be a stable and financially dazzling future ahead of me.

Unfortunately, even if these details were presented to the general public in an uncomplicated form, many individuals would likely find them hard to comprehend. There is a lot of skepticism when it comes to trusting and believing that the governmental system can actually provide monetary gains whereby people's contributions are tax-deductible. Furthermore, any capital gains taxes are due and payable only after the accounts are realized. It's hard to accept as true that the investment is perfectly legal and is an open invitation to anyone eighteen years of age or older to take part in it. Even without having a handbook as a reference point, I engage in conversations with individuals who choose to procrastinate or hold back from entrusting even their most anemic funds to any Retirement Savings Plan. They suspect there will be too much legal jargon to contend with and more often than not, they don't feel up to the game of guessing the right shade of the almighty dollar. For many citizens advancing toward the golden portal, the efforts required to make a financial impact today in order to improve tomorrow leaves them unsure of which system or type of venture would provide the most viable solution.

Feeling too apprehensive to deal with the possibility of finding hidden, complex rules attached to this type of speculation discourages them from doing anything further to explore that avenue. To them, it's preferable to live in denial of what might lie around the corner as long as they can keep their distance from any financial complexities.

Another conceivable explanation for their chronic procrastination could be that by keeping with the status quo, they have something to worry and complain about for the next decade or so. Retirement has not hit their home turf yet; therefore, any step toward this determination is classified either a search for premature distress or an exercise in redundancy.

It's of no surprise that their individual living quarters don't showcase any spontaneous flickers or splashes of ambition.

When the time comes for them to move on with their life, there will be only emptiness in the horizon and no leading roles remotely apparent to them.

Any pro-active person who meets these types of individuals can get carried away writing a pile of reference notes while they observe the lack of enthusiasm being generated from such a crowd. A more enterprising person might easily form the impression that there are no tornados of thoughts stirring within these people's minds with respect to investing in their retirement.

Is the performance of everyone's personal financial accountability, security, welfare, and self-interest open for public opinion? Or, is each one of us bound to act according to what we think is right for us even when our views appear wrong to others? Maybe the winning retirement strategy arrives on the scene saddled with an avalanche of incomplete and deceitful points to test our tolerance for the truth about ageing. I still find that lackadaisical interest in a future financial map can only deny us the legitimacy of a sound retirement package. How can we ignore preparing for the day when work is out of the picture and finances take a different turn? I can only presume that foreign to most of us is the fact that, with a smart twist of financial forethought, we can gain access to unusual values in our life time.

A few years ago, someone of ripe age and sound experience told me that in the pursuance of happily fitting in tomorrow's world with self-sufficiency, one must develop the ability to avoid falling short on the finer and most unassuming concepts of life. When the pain of listening to people ridicule the benefits of a retirement saving plan, my zeal for self-sufficiency overpowers me, and I become more vocal on the subject. To me, the argument represents a piece of life's mystery easy enough to defend.

Being aware of what is financially available as we advance toward a later stage of our being helps us minimize the anonymity that lies ahead. In addition to feeling appeased that we did the right thing for ourselves, it's practical to be prepared to cash-in on any opportunity that comes our way. Financial planning is especially worthwhile if it is designed with the right set of circumstances to improve our knowledge. We should not be fearful or hesitant of aligning our self-control with advanced choices that define our purpose in life.

If we begin with the end in mind, it would be foolish of us to expect a lucky chance to come knocking on our door or remind us to book an appointment to discuss our future plans. It's up to us to solicit the appropriate plan that includes a concrete retirement segment that is made to measure. One should never undermine or underestimate the sheer importance or the muscle of our defensive actions. Those acts are the set-off points that correspond with the correct calculation of allowances for our success or failure in our pensioned years.

Later that afternoon, I sat deep in thought, arms crossed and wearing a frown when I got an unsettling feeling, forewarning me that mayhem would be wreaked if I continued to pout much longer. After I emitted a small whoop, I regained my bearings and put forth a motion to take apart the grumpiness I felt toward what I thought were the imperfections of the world and of life itself. Since I represented a quorum of one for this meeting, I quickly followed the motion with a second. Needless to say, that sensible proposition passed uncontested. There was no room for disputing the purpose of my action and nobody around to be an uncooperative participant.

Another factor I needed to accept was this: The world is made up of different people, some of whom are doers while others are loafers. Most loafers think they are at risk of exploitation. Wondering what passes through their mind on any given day, took more than a moment of thought. Then, I tested my acting skills to see if I could replicate their low-level activities. It wasn't long before I had the obvious answer. I felt a pang of sadness in my stomach, and for the next few days I couldn't stop thinking about it. Sponsored by similar beliefs from scores of contemporaries, it was clear that neither I nor my colleagues would ever entertain the desire to become advocates for the lethargic.

Thomas Jefferson said: "Lethargy is the forerunner of death to the public liberty." How can I rationalize joining rallies in support of those who purposely choose to exhibit defiance toward a good day's work and of financial independence let alone personal classiness? Who can find their selection exciting, funny, or labeled as living in good taste? I consider this feeble and ill- selected option a foolish existence devoid of ambition, depth and direction. In my daily annotation, if you don't know where you want to go in life, it doesn't matter which road you take, or if you move at all; there's a good chance you'll never arrive anywhere. It must be true that there are none as deaf and blind as those who will not hear or see.

As I watched the minutes on the clock ticking away, I couldn't help wondering if the path of our destiny could be seduced into letting us harvest our hearts' desires without having to work for any of it. Perhaps the way we choose to live life can be compared to the hinges on a door. When the door is continuously used, the hinges are oiled and well maintained, the door turns swiftly and quietly, similar to the existence of pro-active individuals. But when the hinges are left unused, they get rusty and noisy, and the door turns very slowly, identical to the loafers' way of life. Fearing I might fall into a state of dismay or even alarm with respect to dissimilar types like the doers and the loafers, I quickly pulled myself together and centered my energy on the task of the day: celebrating my sixty something birthday. I was still unwilling to acknowledge that I should have been prepared and eager to appreciate all the greetings. More to the point, I was entirely accountable for my swiftness in accepting these bighearted wishes.

Uncertain of how to properly deal with this dilemma, or what I should do for the rest of day, I bit my bottom lip and at a snail's pace graduated to biting my fingernails. At the same time, my eyes scanned the periphery for clues on how to find an ideal place for the "what's best to do at my age" symposium. Attempts to find the correct answer came back empty-handed with the exception of the following assertion: I prefer to have an occupation rather than sit back and befriend a rocking chair. I most definitely do not want to start a sedentary relationship with the couch in order to pass the day's hours. Idling has never surfaced as a practical or beneficial selection of daily activity for me. I come alive and do my best work when I have a variety of alternatives twirling around in my head. Some may call this buzz a form of multitasking that has the potential to screw up many things all at the same time. I call it living life with passion and usefulness.

Some people say there can be no denying I'm an advocate of a good balance of work and play. This equilibrium is hard to achieve and is not something to be summarily discarded. I often catch myself wholly rejecting the words "not really" if anyone dares to oppose my theory. When that occasion pops up, I persist and say that if your livelihood is carried out with passion in your heart, then an occupation becomes an excellent source of mental and physical stimulation. Most importantly, I long for the opportunity to have the audience see eye to eye with me when I suggest that employment has the capability to provide an escape from attractions to sedentariness. To me, employment is the classification that delivers the resources for completing an unfinished population.

I feel excited when I come across those rare moments of connection with people who have a mindset that echoes mine – that is, individuals who are happy to live in a world that sometimes gives the impression of being an impenetrable and socially divided place. This is the illustration that depicts my impression of a glazed population.

TIME IS OF THE ESSENCE

All the daylight hours that stretch from dawn to dusk are not long enough to absorb the tension brought by those who overtook my space on this special day.

By the end of the day, the morning's good wishes and constant questions about my retirement status were still weaving in and out of my mind.

How does an individual decide how long to work and what bench-mark should determine when one needs a change of pace? When is an opportune time to initiate a walk toward the exit sign that leads to a place located a light distance away from the work force? This question has the touch of a tough probe that may very well draw different answers from each person facing this test of time. Abandoning the subject for a moment sure seemed like the right thing to do. The next step was to leave contemplation hanging in the balance and continue to play out this day without coming to any serious conclusions.

What I was aiming for was the avoidance of likely getting blindsided by those questions and consequently becoming incapable of hitting on my legitimate meaning of February 24th. Yes, I can now add another year to my life's calendar! I can also proclaim to myself and anyone else willing to take notice that, for me, nothing has changed today. But, I managed only to exhale deeply and nod to myself. Then, attempting to steer away from gloominess, I did what I often do when I'm stuck in a null-and-void trance: I poured myself a strong cup of dark roasted coffee. Then, anxious to admire the outdoor energy, I opened the curtains of my big bay window and sat blankly staring out window.

In the course of provoking numb thoughts to leisurely sabotage my mind, I let my eyes emulate a vari- focal lens requiring no manual or digital adjustment to display a clear exterior view of the area. No transmission set-backs were encountered while broadcasting the finer images of outdoor inactivity. There was no one speaking or gesturing to me. There were no objects in sight, no static or moving figures to be acknowledged, and no creatures lurking nearby. In some ways, this was a real moment in time and not my imagination playing tricks on me. Everything simply stood still. No vehicles moved or whooshed about, no pedestrians were seen walking, no birds chirped and not even the squirrels were awake in search of their favorite nuts or playing catch-me-if you can with each other.

Inside the house, I remained sitting in a daze for a long while. Being cut off from everything helped me keep my head clear of any sound and of any sign of a developing brain-storm. My brain felt useless— I had nothing to write down, nothing to read and nothing to say. I closed my eyes and let myself be overtaken by a weightless feeling of quietude and contentment. The treasured emotion that sprang up out of nowhere made me realize that one can gain personal satisfaction through life's simplest requirements.

Nature has a way of teaching us that it's fine to pass up the unnecessary hunt in the hopes of finding a perfect moment of existence. Conformity will serve us well if only we take the time to read life's labels properly. The biggest label is the one that tells us to be who we are, do what we do best, learn about the things we don't know, and don't try to be someone we're not. This is one of nature's free gifts we often tend to ignore or seldom take the time to analyze, understand, or appreciate.

Pressing myself to escape from a hazy state of mind, I didn't hear the cell phone ring. Although the house was especially quiet at the time, I didn't hear anything. The phone rang several times. When I finally heard it and looked at the identity of the caller, I inexplicably felt a wave of warmth cross my face. I let the call go to voicemail, telling myself I would retrieve the message later and apologize to the caller for not being available. That promise was purposely broken and the call was not returned. I couldn't bear to hear another "are you ready for retirement now?" question. I couldn't recall any other occasion where I dodged answering the phone, but I didn't lose sleep over that particular misdeed.

Notwithstanding my silly state of mind, I gradually came to the realization that, this birthday, meant an exhibition of confidence, the beginning of a new year ahead, and the modest hope for some personal significance. This simple prologue encouraged me to slash away at the dark mood that had visited me in the earlier hours of the day. My adrenaline piped up, and those nagging questions about early retirement no longer felt like intrusions weighing me down. Flooded with eagerness for a resolution, I released a short gasp, ran my hand over my forehead, re-fuelled with a new shimmering attitude, and proceeded to carry on with my original plans for the day. In doing so, I concluded that nobody's subjective opinion would be allowed to dictate what and when my direction for the future should become an article of contention or come under sneering criticism or scrutiny.

Today was one of my yearly special days and I would not be angry with anyone. I might be judged as being a little bold toward some people but not angry. Being angry on my birthday would not be like me. None of these confused emotions are me being me. I don't let frustration gain power over me. I'm the person who turns away from uncertainty and mixed emotions in search of better grounds. This on-the-spot resolve led me straight to the key-holder rack that hung motionless by the front door. With neurotic energy and steady hands, I retrieved the car keys and headed to my vehicle sitting unoccupied in the driveway. It was quietly waiting and ready to oblige any request. Whispering nonsense to myself, I turned the engine on, and without batting an eyelid maneuvered the vehicle away from the driveway and on to the road. I was mindful only of my sheer determination to stay the day's course without dissecting all the stuff that had gone on so far.

I began to drive at uptight speeds, and before long I could feel my breath exhaling in unstable breezes. Adamant to keep going without second-guessing my motive, I pushed myself to wipe out the unexpected morning inquisitions that had come at me without warning and casually carried on as if nothing anyone had said to me had mattered. It was proving to be unnecessarily hard for me to get from the start of the day to the end of it without spewing sarcastic remarks and making salty comments about reaching the age of adult maturity. By dusk, I was ready to take a few steps down memory lane just to put things into proper perspective. As I did so, I shrugged my shoulders and acknowledged how fanatical I've always been about work and having a career, looking good at any age, exhibiting personal charisma, and being an independent individual. Once again, I expressed my unyielding stand on how an occupation can offer the opportunity to seek and seize every available opening in the quest to reach our peak whether visible or imaginary. Age should not play a part in this exchange as long as one has a clear mental capacity and a healthy disposition. The sky is the universe's designated summit point. It is up to us to do whatever it takes to reach our outer limits.

MIXED EMOTIONS

Emotions of Retirement

It was surprising even to me that I had managed to keep my emotions concealed all day long. Most importantly, I had not dropped any anchors simply by being asked about my tomorrows instead of the meaning today ought to have for me. Surely this was not a day to deal with split-seconds of self-doubts or entertain withering thoughts. I'm not sure what I really wanted to do on this day, but it definitely did not include being subjected to any level of grumpiness. This birthday did not come with the gall to deliver lectures on the physics of work or to warn me about consequences brought on by dullness once out of the work scene. But even with such snarls of defiance, I felt those pestering questions about retirement reaffirming they would not go away until I was prepared to offer a reasonable response. I have none to give at this time, not because I'm clueless, but because I don't yet have a levelheaded answer. I'm gracefully avoiding making a failed decision by saying nothing and doing nothing.

What I need now is a little downtime to improve my mind's healthiness so that I can think straight. The absence of getting anything done about a retirement strategy could possibly allow my brain to develop new ideas. I don't mind taking a little extra time-out to be alone with my thoughts. It's not a bad idea to allocate a *little* time for me and my mixed feelings. Throughout the years, I've learned that solitude often can aid in the development of oneself. This savored state of privacy can be branded the director of character identification and can help us realize our true potentials. Life does not have to be non-stop all the time. We need time-out even when the call for relaxing on command does not sit anywhere near the intersection marked "realizable and contentment.' There is always hope that tomorrow or the day or the months after that will open a door to new opportunities and cancel-out indecision. Perhaps then, I'll feel more at ease, knowing I didn't let my current doubts undermine my determination to push ahead with a properly calculated retirement plan when the time is right.

It would be tactless for me to think that after so many years of hearing the tone of my voice sound like a reform warden, I might perhaps let down my guard and risk being caught at a loss for words or resolve. If that were to happen, the peril of allowing a hindrance to sneak in and affect my livelihood would feel like putting the boot to my self-loyalty. The key concern is that I keep my carefully measured decision-making process intact while continuing to sort through my pitiless politics of indecision. I have to make sure I'm not misplacing any possible retirement opportunity.

What does retirement mean anyhow? Could it be a possible obliteration of status in terms of what an individual does for a living? Does it mean that I, like many other baby boomers, will soon be joining the sixteen percent of the population better known to the world as the "graying generation?" Or am I merely one person in the pool of people edging toward a significant age mark? Whether we're rich or poor, healthy or sick, strikingly good looking or not so appealing, thus far, no one has been able to debunk the powerful ageing process. To my knowledge, no one has been able to successfully reverse the ancient vitality known to all of us as the "cycle of life."

It's a proven fact that the life cycle is made up of several important developmental stages.

Today, I will confess that I'm well aware I've been occupying a spot in the mature-adult stage for some fourteen years, and it's time for me to move on to the next phase. I must accept that although I moved from being an adult to becoming a more mature- adult without too much fuss, this latest occurrence leaves me experiencing something that's out of my element. What I should be focusing on is the fact that the most important qualities of life, such as respect, virtuousness, and acquired awareness, will not come to an abrupt end with mature-adulthood. There is no obvious reason for me or anyone else to issue an impromptu statement or a written affidavit in support of ageing denials.

However, the repeated image of seeing myself as a retired woman bewilders my mind. The truth is that this process doesn't give us a chance to doubleback.

So, does being a mature person mean it's time to take a special view of what life is really about? Is it time for me to admit that our existence should not be taken for granted? Is this the day to endorse living life to the fullest so that each one of us can be a significant part of a much bigger picture? This may be a conformist idea, but, I'd bet if we put this practice to the test, we would enjoy the benefits gained. If we take this approach, maybe we can avoid falling into personal shock or suffering from the disappointments associated with "getting older."

There must be an abstract ideal circling somewhere above us that says we, humans, are responsible for believing, accepting, and respecting life's untainted motives. This must hold especially true in evaluating the strength of our daily exercise of bona fide conviction. Although for some of us this may not be a clear motive for wanting to live as long as we can, or qualify life as the greatest myth in the world, it has the power to perplex us all. I'm sure we all experience life moments when we're called to act or to resolve a difficult situation whether we're up for it or not.

On the surface, we may think we've been dealt a heavy blow and cannot work the situation out by ourselves, but, we know, we can always connect with our central voice for support and consolation. The rule of thumb for addressing daily challenges, life skills, and the gracefulness of ageing, can be guided by our inner arbiter. Each passing day teaches us this lesson.

By now, I'm almost an expert at handling diverse phases and transitions in life. I say this for the simple reason that, over the years, I had to absorb many adversities and make numerous adjustments in the course of developing my business. I've become adept at treating the sales and administrative staff as important fundamentals of my company's and, ultimately, my life cycle. On the other hand, my personal ageing process is uncommon to me and, by far, a more difficult test to get ahead of. This fragmented turmoil kept my emotions off-balance and, for the time being, everything remains loosely woven together. To forecast a realistic turning point, I need to put in proper context not only my life's personal particulars but my business theories and practices. Following that, I'd need to do my most excellent work and correctly interpret the evidence available to me.

This "planning for the days ahead" requires me to work out the legitimacy of my retirement, and do some training for a new and slower pace. The groundwork also calls for self-control, creativity and clear thinking.

After considerable evaluation of these points, I realized that my sought-after exit strategy needs a considerable amount of time to assemble it properly and to digest the relative information. But here is another interesting point: This project can easily exceed the allotted space I've marked on my current day-timer.

Today, I face a test of gigantic responsibility. For a few hours, I've become the perfect embodiment of a person struggling to get her head out of a foggy haze. Still, I'm not prepared to imply that my present hesitation is proof of disbelief or disloyalty toward life's natural progression. I'm familiar with the advantages of viewing this evolutionary period as a gradual, if ambivalent personal work-out.

Apart from trying to gulp down disbelief about my retirement psychoanalysis, a few days after this, the federal government saw fit to play its part. In the name of public service, Social Service Canada had the postman deliver a recycled brown envelope addressed to me personally. Just thinking of what the letter might contain became my distressing wake-up call of the day. The sight of this package caused my vision to be unfocused, making everything around me a blur. Once my eyes cleared (with the help of vision glasses), I was able to confirm that I had, received my ***pension application.*** That wicked letter contained a lot more than a couple of retirement thoughts written in a readable prose. The content of the enclosure was like an enema filled with detailed questions sent to assist and direct me through the transitional steps. Besides finding all the irritating information unfamiliar, I can further describe it as something less than inspirational. But those forms spoke of the facts as they were. It was up to me to come to terms with my new reality.

Struggling to move forward in some semblance of composure, I realized I was being overtaken by the anxiety that made this a turbulent period in my life. I became so irritated with this new predicament that I felt the urge to scream "code red" if only to bring my panic under control. But there were no interested parties available to receive my distress call. On second thought, I decided not to act on that frightening impulse and took a less intense approach. My resolve was to revert to life's rule number one: avoid trepidation. If I skipped over this self-imposed strife, I stood a good chance of alleviating my distress. Minutes later, however, I still couldn't find an acceptable answer to clear my confusion, and my animated thoughts bordered obsession. The good news is that I had an open-door invitation to exchange a few words with my two children and my husband regarding this bizarre moment. After all, isn't that what family members are for? Yes, indeed! That is exactly what family is about.

Although, family might represent only a small unit of our society, the word is very important and has significant meaning. Family is the group one goes to for support and to feel sheltered and secure. Family members are the people we can count on whether the circumstances are social, economic, or personal. This type of hospitality may not hold true for some unfortunate people whose family affiliates behave more like a cactus plant. It may sound a bit extreme, but those family members consistently fail to make a better difference because they only know to welcome their relatives with a sharp verbal prick. Then there are those members who provide support for each other in a totally different, direct, and unfiltered manner.

With reference to the latter, there is the story of an elderly couple who went to a theatre and half way through the movie, the husband whispered to his wife: "Maggie, I think I just let out a non-smelly, silent fart." His wife promptly answered: "Oren, I think you should first trim your nose hairs so you can actually have a sense of smell, and then get new batteries for your hearing aids." There is no debating the fact that support or the lack thereof, has different meanings for different folks. Here begs the question: Is the public space of our family's morals being besieged by bafflement?

Despite all these debatable behaviors, I felt sure I had come to know my immediate family quite well over the years. It was not by coincidence that I could anticipate what their likely response to my retirement quandary might be. As I stood grinding my teeth as if to pulverize my tension, I could do no more than envision their smirks. Then a text message from my daughter grabbed my attention. A subsequent note was immediately thereafter received from my son. As expected, both wrote that I was misconstruing a natural progression for an imagined attack on my persona. To my children, my decision to retire or semi-retire seemed like a risk-free choice with no potential for vulnerable results or costly consequences. They looked at this event as a healthy walk in the park with no reason for panic. More than anything else, I saw this as an uplifting moment that brought back my coherence. I knew they would be entirely supportive of whatever decision I made. They would be there for me whether I chose to defer retirement for the time being or whether I decided to take a second look at what it had to offer. However, both of them reminded me that I was not a good candidate for full retirement yet.

My next step was to drop debating the pros and cons of retirement and run outside where my husband was working to show him the letter. That split-second decision was not an act open to explanation; this was serious business. Amidst the commotion, I nearly lost sight of the fact that contrary to my not-so-positive excitement about retirement, my husband had long anticipated his own. He had been elated when he finally received his application. He was even more overjoyed when that pledge was backed by his pension allowance, which arrived at the door right on time. He had not been willing to work a day longer than his sixty-fifth birthday. He most definitely did not wish to continue working until his eyesight required stronger bifocals to help him look down before he stepped off a curb or out of the car to make sure his feet touched the ground. I also found fascinating his level of appreciation for the parting gift his employer had presented to him on his last day of work. He was given a Bulova watch.

What good was a watch now that he no longer had to monitor time? Maybe, they were sending him off with a reminder that time had advanced very fast? Maybe it was an omen of how fast his years of service had gone by. Whatever their good intention might have meant, he had been thrilled to add this watch to his pre-existing collection that included an Omega, a Timex, a Seiko, and a Citizen timepiece. You wouldn't find any cobwebs covering those pieces, but I know they've just been sitting motionless in his drawer. Not to my surprise, he saw my distress as a comical charade not deserving of a great deal of attention. His response may not have been deliberately hurtful, but obviously I hadn't scored any points here. I tried to look at my dilemma from his point of view, but my pluck seemed to slide into the washbasin of life's reality. I was not having a stellar day today!

It must be true that not all people are cut from the same fabric. I didn't need to jog my memory to acknowledge that fundamental dissimilarities can seldom be accepted as a good source of laughter or rounds of fun. I'm mindful that my husband greatly enjoys his retirement and does his best to give a solid meaning to the phrase "golden years."

What does the phrase "golden years" make reference to? Does it mean that a person who has reached the age of sixty-five should readily embrace a new way of life? Does it characterize the people who have reached the peak of their achievements? Or did someone use this terminology as a campaign slogan to advertise a time when one can collect pension benefits, receive social security and cash-in their investments? Perhaps it's just a reference to the song "Golden Years" released in 1975 by David Bowie. He sings about sticking with his partner for a thousand years and nothing was going to touch her in those golden years. In other words, was he saying that if we live past retirement age and are still healthy and of sound mind, we should cherish each of our days ahead because every day is worth gold?

Shortly thereafter, both my children delivered a similarly amusing comment "your distress signal is hilarious!" Seriously? They were having genuine fun with age jokes and laughing at my dilemma. Obviously, no shockwave-recovery efforts would emanate from that much younger meadowland any time soon. It was time for me to concede that the world did not stop because the package containing an unanticipated, bitter-sweet document had suddenly arrived at my door. What a day of folly this was turning out to be. I wasn't sure whether to light a few sparklers in honor of the past busy years, or, light a candle in anticipation of the slower paced years to come. Maybe fireworks would be the solution that could iron out things today without pondering the past or fretting about the future.

THE QUEST FOR SERENITY

Emotions of Retirement

The pathway leading to retirement consolation may not be equally smooth or easy to trek for everyone. Without a doubt, the rhythm for traversing life's different cycles does not stop, nor does it reverse gear because some of us get a pounding feeling in our chest when the progression of ageing becomes apparent. It may be next to impossible to figure out the meaning of many things, but the ability to understand the circle of life appeals to many people. Conversely, the world is home to many others who see it as an inflexible drama unfolding before their eyes. Maybe life is like the illusion of a transparent photo image.

Outwardly, I did not have the courage to show signs of concern, antipathy, or even confusion over the matter. This held especially true while in the company of those who had willfully and joyously opted for early retirement and those who happily retired at the age of sixty-five. Inwardly, my nerves were busy battling a different kind of confused complexity. With each strained breath taken inconspicuous to the crowd, I could feel the sound inside my chest bounce around in a woozy blur. As I heard others speak about their retirement with gleaming enthusiasm, I tried to figure out what they all had in common. Obviously, none of them seemed to suffer from any malice or bitterness as a result of their transition. Could it be that I needed to sleep this listlessness away before I made myself the sore subject of squandered hope and happiness? There must be a less complicated and more convincing explanation. Is it possible the correct answer is kept hidden from the general public? Is it only made apparent to a select few who have a highly calibrated retirement approval level? It may sound unreal, but without warning, the confusing atmosphere between my thoughts and reality gave me the feeling that the room was growing blistering hot. Why was this happening to me? Was I selfishly waiting for an answer to drop down from the sky and hit me over the head?

I asked myself this questions: "Am I an odd person loitering on the side-lines of those individuals who more easily have made sense of ageing?" The obvious answer was not so hard to find once I was willing to start looking for it. In my pursuit of fact findings for the ageing society, I came across a statement that addressed the cultural phenomenon of the baby boomers who are turning sixty or sixty-five years of age worldwide. Apparently, these double-digit birthdays are happening at a rate of almost eight thousand a day. *What a party this must be!* In Canada alone, we are seeing a massive demographic shift because we have more people over the age of sixty-five than young children under the age of fifteen. Could we be facing labour issues in years to come? Is Canada hoping that boomers continue to work past their age of retirement in order to maintain the status-quo; thus, delay collecting their pension benefits?

All this could well denote that public officials will have serious theorizing and hefty explaining to do to appease the wondering population. In fact, most of us are already speculating about it. It appears to be plausible that the new generation will be faced with slower economic growth accompanied by the danger of lower standards of living. What will the consequences of a looming slower economic growth mean for the new generation? Will it mean a downward financial trend? Will young workers be saddled with more taxes and less public services? Will having an open-door policy to young immigrants and delaying boomer retirement really help Canada stave-off economic stagnation?

Mathematical estimations reveal that within the next ten to fifteen years we could be looking at ten retirees for each new candidate joining the work force. To do nothing to thwart or battle these seemingly lopsided potential outcomes might just be an exhibition of overconfidence that says, "I warned you about these imminent results." If such predictions are lining up with industrial and commercial business realities, we could be faced with a burdensome bottom line for the country's economic situation in the not-so-distant future. It would seem right to jump in early and stonewall every probable confusion as well as squash any fear of potential fiscal disarray if the powers-to-be act quickly, swallow hard, and engage in vigorous calculus distinctions capable of delivering the appropriate reforms. In my estimation, these reforms cannot be achieved solely through cost- cutting measures impersonating valid solutions.

Often, these short-changed and modernistic solutions are sold to the public by leaders capable of delivering hopeful speeches with a long streak of misinformation. Further, I would argue that history has shown us time and again that successful restructuring cannot be attained solely by curtailing research and development incentives, willfully accepting economic stagnation, downgrading pension payments, or even by diminishing medical and social programs. The past is a teacher whose lessons cannot be obscured let alone silenced. It took our predecessors too long and too much effort combined with utter ardor and absolute determination to advance this far and accomplish so much. How can anyone, not to mention those in the political sphere, support the notion that the true nature of capping or curtailing regime spending on social services is more essential than actually providing well-balanced, short-term, and long-term solutions?

It has occurred to me on many occasions that the infrastructure pitching the governments' fiscal commitment comes pre-equipped or is purposely rigged with a gear that drives in reverse instead of forward. As the impending authenticity for political solutions keeps stalking the unsuspecting population, I am willing to bet that this slow moving federal as well as provincial financial vehicle will eventually emerge with a gearshift marked with an "STC" sticker meaning a "slow transitioning concept" is in progress. "STC" is also the short-form for a political virtue called *"shit on that concept."*

Yes, I do anticipate difficult times ahead coupled with hard and onerous governmental choices. There is no discounting the possibility of seeing threats of skepticism flying around us like dust in the wind. It would be a well thought-out and non-alarming suggestion for some elected officials to come up with sound tidal waves of positive actions. Such deeds might even give them reason to justify their political employment. They would be considered shrewd not to use their status as a self-awarded personal privilege while the rest of the population scuttles for practical answers. To avoid distancing themselves from public economical and financial actuality, I think these leaders need to reach out for more public input. It is important that they redirect the mass of lamentable social conditions to a level that appeases the middle-class citizens instead of appealing and romancing only the wealthy lobbyists. This initial step would undoubtedly be a point in their favor and may help them dodge some heated disagreements. Generally speaking, the civic audience expects no more and no less than the clear facts from smooth political operators. All these officials need to do is to deliver on their promises just like a well written magazine article delivers its narrative. It might be a bit cheeky to suggest that most people's brains are quite capable of making a distinction between fiction and reality, but it's true. Whether it's the working citizens or the unemployed or the retirees, all we're really looking for is the political storytellers to come to terms with the nation's problems and explain how they propose to follow through with practical solutions. Surely it's understood that resolving an issue requires definition, research, evaluation, and a good selection of alternatives that will bring change and improve present circumstances. Their next step should be to brainstorm and figure out if the new approach will lay the foundation for short-term or long-term solutions and what, if any, is the extent of the risk associated with the change.

Let's not forget that some decades ago; it was the baby boomers who dared to force the hand of change for outdated traditions, customs, work ethics, culture and dynamic illustrations. Their efforts were carried out all for the purpose of realizing an important dream. Put differently, every pre-established custom became a subject of questionable behavior or an object in need of modification. In doing so, they illuminated the path to world changes. Their ideals and tough work have paved the way for their own and our personal gains, freedoms, idealism, political and social realism, higher standards of living, and most of all, "financial stability." Hurrah, to the baby-boomers, the generation who has now moved forward and reached a hard-earned and well-deserved retirement juncture that is mediated between personal possessions, entrepreneurship, and adulthood contentment.

The boomers have earned the satisfaction of being able to loosen up their nerves that at times were nastily tested by some arrogant associate or duty superior who frequently managed to tick them off. Now, these retirees have the frankness to tell any unwelcome person of authority to piss-off without the fear of losing their job.

THE BOOMERS' WAY

I am a baby boomer. I am one of those millions of babies who populated the world between 1946 and 1964. These were the years that carried the solemn declaration that rejoicing and reconstructing were the fundamental requirements for achieving genuine progress and citizens' rights. Boomers are the people product of post World War ll. Nineteen forty-five and nineteen forty-six was the time that saw many of the troops who survived the war make good on whatever courage they had managed to conceal during their hope- obscured and war-stricken days. Their anticipation for survival that previously had seemed to abandon them, now rallied around them with an optimistic feeling of being re-energized. At the same time, the end of the war tapped into a sense of joyfulness for the soldiers who would be returning home to their loved ones. The war had viciously robbed them of nearly all their possessions and sometimes had also taken control of their mental space. Many of the surviving soldiers were cautiously enthusiastic to return home with a rehabilitated sense of hope to counter their past misery. Their anticipation for a better and more wholesome future came fortified by the optics that washed away the murky hardships they had endured in the past years. They were not quitters because they had been injured or because they were down. Instead, they returned home equipped with intense aspirations and new plans for a better life. As a result, those plans produced an abundance of favorable results for most of the people. The years passed in better form and all the eagerness and passion for renewed optimism worked out very well for them.

Consequently, many new marriages were celebrated. New nuptials gave way to large numbers of family units springing up everywhere, just as it was intended. Infants' cries and children's laughter caught everyone's ears like the sound of music emanating from the local battery-run radios. Makeshift playgrounds were being built every day, cobblers could hardly satisfy the demands for shoes, young mothers became instant seamstresses, fathers busied themselves growing sufficient provisions for their family, and teaching became the profession of great demand. Schools soon became filled with children ready to learn how to read and write. Just about every parent or guardian denounced illiteracy and innumeracy. Most were so eager to promote mental and social stimulation for their young ones that at times they liberally discouraged and skirted their children from any physical drudgery. In general, a new kind of populace was emerging. The days of the baby boom was asserting its presence worldwide. All those advanced measures had an inexplicable and mysterious quality that to a lot of people felt like a life-altering windfall. On occasion, they could not believe how their hemmed-in personal story could be part of such an innovative and startling broader political and economic spectrum.

This new emergence soon awoke serious interest in the awaiting enterprising developers who had a keen eye for business progress. With thanks to their deep pockets, they were able to purchase suburban land so they could profit from building and selling much needed affordable housing to the newly emergent families. Land developers like W.J. Levitt wasted no time in starting to mass-produce partially factory- assembled, unpretentious looking houses that were cost effective. This creative pursuit successfully enticed potential new owners to reach out and achieve their life's dream. Further, industries that produced electrical or chemical products such as radios, washing machines, air conditioning units, televisions, and a number of chemical products used to aid in the rehabilitation of the agricultural industry saw continued prosperity throughout those post-war years.

The United States, fortunately not having suffered too many staggering losses during the war, supplied first-aid assistance. They also made great financial contributions toward the rebuilding of decimated communication systems and roads within countries freed from the Nazi regime. The U.S. designed a co-operative economic reconstruction program with European countries in order to fend-off useless competition from communist countries. Another reason for this arrangement was the anticipation of speeding up the European economic recovery thereby negating the likelihood of communist intrusion. All this activity came with the assurance to the suburban population that improved road conditions, creation of new highways, the building of new local shopping malls, and medical facilities were in the works and ready to make a dominant impact on their new lifestyles.

Things were beginning to look and feel good for the general population. It was suggested that the difficulties of the past did not need to be re-told too many times. There was a strong desire to believe that the old complexities that had led up to the war, and the consequences people suffered during and after the war, would be life-lessons learned and understood for a very long time. This history lecture would be handed out as the manual of formal instructions meant to educate and caution future generations not to replicate warfare. Otherwise, they would set themselves up for similar hardships at their own personal costs.

We must not overlook the fact that during World War ll, due to their intention of defeating the advancing Germans, the U.S. and much of Europe saw fit to be allied with Russia. However, after the war, the U.S. worried that Russia would soon start spreading communism. A Marshal Plan was devised to begin the healing and help Europe rebuild strong and fast. At the same time, the U.S. wanted to avoid the potential risk of Europe falling under communist dominance. The U.S. did not look favorably at the possibility that Europe might fall prey to governance where the government owned and controlled most of the properties, roads, transportation, agriculture, education, etc. There was obvious concern that if Communism gained momentum, there would be little or no room left for private ownership. Then, in nineteen forty-eight, after much controversy and intense deliberation, the U.S. approved an expenditure of approximately ten billion dollars and moved forward to stimulate economic production in Europe which had been badly destroyed during the war and needed help to rebuild. The U.S. also offered Russia and its eastern allies financial aid as a gesture of diplomacy, but it was turned down.

Within a few years, Western Europe showed solid recovery complimented by a flourishing economic boom. Coal and steel production was another great booster for the European success. Eastern Europe, however, was not as successful even though it met the same economic amalgamating response as Western Europe. Some would suggest this was as a result of the stubborn controls manifested by communist parties. Along with this calibrated progress came large corporations who considered money and prosperity their closest and most trusted allies. It is worth noting how rapidly their aggressive materialistic skills became the essence that created padded financial gratification with little risk of failure for them. Their profits were real and their balance sheet showed no delusions. These masters knew how to play a good hand of business poker while withholding the royal flush for their final round as they drew close to each project's finish line. Union members were promised sensible wages along with long-awaited benefits. Consumer goods were priced within people's means, and the returning soldiers were given subsidized, low-cost mortgages. Times for growth and prosperity were looking matchless, and life offered buoyancy. In real-life meaning, this continuous growth depicted the suburbs as the best place to be, and thus, they quickly became the centre of the population growth.

Baby boomers had a lot of hope and personal promise ahead of them. But as is often the case, after a number of years, not everyone shared the same feeling for this cheerfulness or glowing fulfillment. Some of the women found the suburban lifestyle dissatisfying, although the settings were considered almost perfect for a young family with a level of ambition for a brighter future. These women preferred a more enjoyable and more actively social city life. This might have been one of the factors that contributed to the revival of the feminist interest groups of the nineteen-sixties.

As people began to search for a new pathway to bring fulfillment into their life, it stood to reason that if the status quo lingered in the picture too long, it would also hold true for the period's population growth. Change was now imminent. Change is capable of being good even if doesn't take us where we think we want to go. It opens the window to new opportunities. If by chance, we choose to ignore its calling, change may very well succeed by default.

And so it happened, after almost twenty years of continued population growth, that Dr. Gregory Goodwin Pincus, an American biologist and researcher from New Jersey, co-invented the birth control pill and, with that, he altered and revolutionized those exceedingly family-building dynamics. A new norm was born. Contraception gave rise to an improvement in women's spirits by allowing them increased control over their family life and changed the way relationships were viewed.

By the nineteen-sixties, social uprising led to the sexual revolution and prevented a great number of unwanted pregnancies. There is no doubt a new milestone had been reached. Eight years later, a new intrauterine device (IUD) was approved by the Food and Drug Administration (FDA), and it captured a fair market share. However, by nineteen-seventy, some health issues were becoming apparent to a number of women. The feminist movement did not hesitate to challenge the safety of both birth-control methods. Its hard work soon gave rise to a less intrusive and much safer formulation of contraceptives.

The pathway to change has no end. Unfortunately, even today, there are still over two hundred million women without access to any form of pregnancy prevention. A lot of work remains to be done. Although in general, we have made tremendous strides from the goings on experienced in Europe during the Middle Ages or in ancient China. In those days, women were deemed the sole party responsible for avoiding pregnancy. It is believed that in Europe between the fifth and fifteenth centuries, women had to tie a weasel's testicle to their thighs or around their neck to steer clear of conception. In Ancient China, concubines were known to have drunk lead and mercury to prevent pregnancy. This haphazard mixture was effective enough to cause serious side effects such as sterility, brain damage, and sometimes death.

In the nineteen seventies, change was more impartial, less fate-filtered, and more balanced. It brought some people out of their dormant state and forced them to develop new insights about life.

As the years went by and the young boomers grew up, they developed a cultural curiosity that differed from the older generation. With a lot of curiosity and a flair for the new, these youngsters went in search of more social and civil liberties. True, not all boomers carried the banner of change, but those who fostered that mind-set pushed many buttons to achieve a free- spirited life style inclusive of women's rights, gay rights, and the freedom to choose abortion. They openly protested wars. Some took to flagging their war protests by burning the U.S. flag and then moved to Canada to express their objections. Others grew their hair as a result of breaking with conservative traditions. Some went on to seek-out some measure of monetary success, figuring that money was the answer to everything. Then there were those who didn't fancy living on the edge and, consequently, fell into despair, deeming their life futile because of the ongoing political corruption and unjust oppression.

Daily efforts for change pushed their way through time. Significant progress was slowly being made in a number of areas such as revamping the labour force, updating the education system, supporting the scientific field, and venturing into space. Evolution and its usual selection of randomly occurring transformations managed to change things from their simple form to more intricate structures. High-ranking inspiration joined by a rhapsody of emotions symbolized the general population's endorsements of newly discovered environments. Even the judicial system endeavored to do a little house cleaning. They slowly brought to an end their infamous bravado acts of ridiculing female attorneys at every encounter. That colossal and long- overdue accomplishment stood out as a win for the "new team."

Credit bureaus were starting to feel excluded from world changes, and to avoid facing, or suffering from, "emancipation tardiness," gradually softened their unprecedented practice of denying women economic sovereignty. The new team had scored a second glorious win. Now, women had the right to endorse a cheque! In some cases, women could even sign for a lease and it would be recognized by society as a legal and proper document. *Change is upstanding!*

Change is especially meaningful when people accept it, understand it, and move on without regret or holding a grudge. By now, old controls were inching their way out as women started to contribute to society in ways that were so far removed and unimaginable only a few decades earlier. The age of a new norm was being formed. An irrevocable genre meaning had come alive. Innovative societal trends were being correctly classified as the new standards. However, all this movement did not totally solve the world's problems. It did, nevertheless manage to accomplish a lot of new communal recognitions.

Before long, patience was becoming a virtue as some hard luck was befalling the fearless baby boomer activists. It was not uncommon for their actions to be met with unduly harsh punishment. They frequently were given prison sentences and faced banishment from their employer. Over and over again, even their family members saw fit to ostracize them. All that bitterness did not slow them down because the boomers believed the act of punishing their free spirit was a result of the dread for change. In fact, the movement picked up speed at unprecedented levels even if the officials were not willing to assist them. Their belief and passion for reform was so strong they repeatedly faced whatever aggression or punishment was thrown their way without fear or intimidation. They stood firm on their statement that change was an essential component for the advancement of human kind. With change, they saw opportunities. Opportunities represented the backbone, and the solid substance needed to accomplish different aspects of life. It was their strong desire for change that drove these activists to be unquestioningly ready and willing to continue their disobedience toward the existing laws of the land. Eventually, the unrelenting power of the boomers' actions spilled over and became the unwritten universal lesson of those tempestuous and turbulent years. It would be right to suggest that a sharp tutorial had taken place in the social structure.

Although I was not an actual revolutionary participant, I credited those activists with being razor-sharp individuals having a purpose and a mission to accomplish. Their striking determination made a difference not just for them, but for the new generation at large. Even if I didn't spend every moment of the day dwelling on the situation, my inner spirit hoped and prayed they would have the strength to keep it together for as long as it was necessary. Their strength made it possible for me to imagine a better economic, political, and interpersonal connecting system that brought betterment all through the world.

The time to administer a better classification of individuals and superior ethics was long overdue. Progression toward this worthwhile pinnacle was slow in materializing, but the radicals' willpower was never shortened admiration for the depth of their groundbreaking resolve. I, for one, faithfully followed their actions and learned as much as I could about their tenacity to overcome any set-backs. These radical individuals were prepared to continue accepting and dealing with whatever invasive and relentless personal restraints were handed down to them. None of them expected congratulations, nor did they ask for a pat on the back in recognition of their inspiration.

These are the people who deserve to be remembered as the title holders of moral esteem and fair dealings. They struggled for their novel ideals in every sense of the word and, in the end, they managed to leave a significant imprint in my personal history handbook. Every now and again, I refer to the same handbook of reference of the earlier period if only to reminisce and appreciate the scores of remarkable moments that took place during those years. In doing so, I cannot help but feel a touch of melancholy creeping into my stomach. It's amazing to recall seeing how the reform seekers scored a number of goals for their team.

They chose to never take their eyes off the main objective even when the continued unrest labeled them "lost souls" and greeted them with a kick in the teeth. Those troubling conditions enforced by bigotry were by no means victorious in breaking the new mold. In fact, it was the boomers' mold that broke the world's silence in order to create a more open-minded and less restrictive and segregated life style. Through their unrelenting efforts for change, women were no longer expected to be limited to being good homemakers, gays were no longer told to stay out of society's space, and education was an open business for everyone's gain. The boomers' loyalty and drive toward emancipation kept them looking forward for even more political and social adjustments. They refused to look back and remind themselves of how hollow everything had been for them in the past.

Their task at hand required remorseless personal endurance, and they manifested their steadfastness by opening their hearts and minds to the lyrics transmitted from radios and jukeboxes whenever and wherever it was possible. Music, for them, was the network connection to the outside world. Through music they found the confidence to fortify their self-esteem. The melodies acted as a stress releaser, appeased their soul, and boosted emotional brainpower. They found gratification especially from the songs of great musical artists like Frank Sinatra, Nat King Cole, the Beatles and many others. In 1957, Elvis Presley effectively caught their ear with his songs, "Jail House Rock" and "All Shook Up." The Everly Brothers spread a lot of good cheer with "Wake Up Little Susie." In 1969, Led Zeppelin brought harmony to the boomers with "Whole Lotta Love" followed by "Only You," released in 1973 by the Platters. Music was the baton that touched everyone.

Today, this may sound like a bit of a stretch, but to the reformers, music was the wholesome therapy that got them through many tough times and brought distinct happiness and meaning into their daily lives. Their truism was being heard, and to some extent, even frivolously accepted. To most boomers, yesterday represented a period of time gone by; the present was at all times open for reform, and tomorrow promised to be a day to celebrate their accomplishments. Tomorrow pledged to arrive with a memento to remember the thrashing around these reformers had been subjected to. Tomorrow would also ensure that plenty of streamers would be free-flying to celebrate the end of their past intolerant days.

The birth of more approachable social days and their significance could not be denied any longer. There would be no more round-table debates about the need for emancipation and no insignificant discussions about "what once was."

Reminiscing about my younger years left the distinct impression that those days, months, and years, had gone by too fast. Time seemed to have run away without anyone noticing. So far, I have kept my promise to never forget those past, deep-seated radical principles. Instead, I replay their value in my head constantly and without doubts. I cannot let the heroics of yesteryears slip from my grasp or become rusty and devoid of meaning. I'm determined to keep this subdivision of my memory alive and hope that the effects give a different meaning to the word "insuperable."

Without the past, I would not have had the opportunity to be the woman I am today. I'm open to carrying on with my personal and business life without the danger of being ostracized from society or feeling trapped in a world of female abandon. It's due to the boomers' push to eradicate many unduly restricted boundaries that has made it possible for me to catch a break in my adult life. It is because of their hunger for change that I had the opportunity to freely administer with gratitude, delight and poise in my chosen career. The radical boomers are owed a lot of credit for their initiatives.

The artificial premise, however, that all types of reforms occur for a good reason does not come as a shock to me nor does it ring true to my ears. I am not so sheltered to become oblivious to the fact that even back then, some reform-seekers did not hesitate to venture into a number of serious missteps. When an opportunity for making money presented itself, some became instantly energized and dangerously obsessed with making the most of what they saw as a scintilla of hope to satisfy their egotism. Their self- inflated personalities sometimes led them to believe they were more economically attuned and far superior to many other citizens. This was especially true when their eager ambitions, combined with a not-so-moderate business plan, enhanced their odds for success and produced considerable sums of money. Through their cleverly crafted accounting methods, a number of boomer entrepreneurs made the ranking of "culpable parties" responsible for the evaporation of many, many millions of dollars. Such cohesive financial activities not only took the government officials and the collection agencies by surprise, but rumor has it that it left them wallowing in disappointment. Those practices did not discriminate between the two groups of money grabbers, thus making the proceedings equally intoxicating for tax collectors and third party agencies.

Authorized collectors often found themselves caught in a web of deceptions secretly pioneered by skilled business masterminds who could not help scoff at officials as soon as they turned their backs. It has been mentioned many times that the boomers' dexterity delivered a serious blow to the government's budget in the late 1970s and 1980s. Their nimbleness left authorities baffled and at a sober disadvantage as they watched themselves be genially swindled out of their anticipated revenue. Barring a few troublesome issues, someone was always ready to outfox the governing party, and they often discretely celebrated the outcome of their innovative presentations.

Sadly for authorities, these were not the kind of thunderous results the revenue department had predicted, or, imagined they had to count on. On many occasions, these diverse industry instigators dared the bothersome government to try and match wits with them by facing-off in a different and new-fangled business reality. They were not naïve, but the government officials knew, figuratively speaking, they had been mugged by speculative and spiteful perpetrators. At times, even when the end result did not work out, the message to the authorities was still delivered with the same gusto and clarity: Either step up your game or get out of our way.

Boomers took great pride in the preservation of their mysteriously covert business formula and cautiously kept it shielded and hidden away from the authorities' reach. Throughout the years, they challenged the then present rule-based laws and introduced different forms and methods of income practices, leadership initiatives, and administrative concepts.

Individuals who cleverly managed to accumulate substantial affluence became cunningly eager to make donations in support of their political party of choice. Without a hint of hesitation, or a second thought, they attended rallies to make sure industrialization and education would not become forgotten promises. After all, what good can come from promises without performance? These citizens were not in the least interested in paying attention to any artificial explanations or to a litany of excuses for broken political promises.

Boomers who did not possess these unique personality traits were by no means cast aside. Their dissimilar approach to life did not go unnoticed and not too many things were known to be off-boundaries to them. They too, showcased courage and enthusiasm even though they projected a different kind of ability to deal with difficult situations without surrendering to fear. One of the things their dynamic interest for betterment led them to do was to venture into real- estate ownership. With whatever little monetary savings they could afford, they purchased their first home. Once the first purchase was comfortably safeguarded against the outstanding mortgage, they continued on with the same unrelenting ambition and excitement to purchase a second and sometimes even a third home for rental income purposes.

It has been speculated that in the course of doing so, they probably managed to drive the cost of the housing market way up. Higher housing cost was a two pronged fork that benefitted some parties by promoting healthier assets while colliding with others by posing a difficult start if they did not have the capacity to come up with the elevated start-up cost. This unprecedented situation may not have been a deliberate assault on the less fortunate, but its radical continuation did not become everyone's success story either.

THE FINANCIAL GPS

Being a baby boomer, I have always preferred to follow the GPS (Global Position System) of fiscal responsibility, and I continue to stay on the side of caution when financial outlay is part of the plan. I consider fiscal literacy a theory that works best when put into practice. Today, I still don't particularly see how the rise in the housing costs of the 1970's and 1980's was a tremendously difficult state of affairs. I don't think I'm nuts when I say I hardly believe such volatility became a real threat to the longevity of real estate-growth. Not too many people in my circle tend to agree with my views. For some individuals, my justification that such monetary gains were a reflection of the boomers' intuitive work does not ring true. Even my argument that their wealth came as a result of the proceeds received from risky investments does not hold water in their narrow mindset. At times, we get so drawn in that we let these contentious debates go on and on until I decline to further explain my hypothesis.

The awkward thing is that my associates only see my squabbles as a courtship of poor excuses for the boomers' success stories and not as matter clarification or scope enlightenment. Since the well to-do, the less affluent, the industrialist, the capitalists, the economists, and the non-interested parties will forever occupy a spot in our circle of life, someone will always be held responsible for the final outcome.

Although I understand that some people's winning accounts were destiny re-aligned, there is one open question that frequently buzzes through my mind: Is most of the boomers' money and asset accumulation carried out in anticipation of procuring financial stability for their senior years, or are the majority of my contemporaries counting on passing this amassed fortune on to their children? If their plan is solely to procure for their children regardless of their age or income levels, I'm curious to find out how many parents actually feel confident enough that their children have the ability to correctly manage their inheritance. Nowadays, there is visible evidence that an unnerving number of parents who own a financial cushion still continue to monetarily bail out their children on demand, and they do it without so much as a whisper to the contrary. In my unsolicited opinion, this can only add up to a negative path headed away from our personal boundaries of responsibility.

I think that if we were to make a positive presumption about the boomers' financial literacy and astute saving methods, we can say with confidence that the more enlightened ones have the talent and the vision to allocate sufficient funds with which to achieve dual objectives. Subsequent to being a vocal participant in many of these controversial discussions, I know I may not have too many allies left, but the ones I do have, think the way I do. Firstly, we find it important to make arrangements to maintain a healthy income when our time to collect a government pension arrives. Secondly, we are happy to believe that because of our prudent fiscal management of past years, we can now spare a few dollars for our children's welfare.

Although I am not about to choke on any sobs that some of us got it right, I'll say it feels good to take for granted that we get a passing check mark. Still, none of these thoughts provided me with a clear response to my unanswered questions for an exit strategy.

I felt a ghostly hand on my shoulder as I stood bereft of what to do next, wondering why decision making is easier when it centres on others. Relying on my own imagination, something grabbed my attention, and it came to me: I should try to figure out how my colleagues managed to arrive at their decision to retire so freely. Perhaps it had happened by way of an intuitive process.

Maybe it was achieved through reasoned calculations. Maybe, it took a little of both. I just could not find the right angle from which to tackle this unrelenting difficulty. Why could I not stay focused long enough to figure out my best course of action to pull off a satisfying retirement arrangement? To do nothing about a given situation is not the best decision I've ever made, but in this instance, doing nothing was my decision non-the-less.

I turn on the television set in an effort to divert my thoughts away from the retirement itch huddled in the front lobe of my head. I really had to find a way to clear that irritating itch I can't seem to scratch. Was there a secret retirement blueprint to uncover? If so, what directions was I missing?

Shortly thereafter, it occurred to me that the plausible option for a semi-retirement or full retirement selection would not voluntarily come to meet me with a big smile and a loud bang. It was obvious that I had to do some maintenance work with my inner alliances before I could pinpoint the most likely answer. While I relish the ability to work my own schedule and be the one in charge of managing my business' financial activities among other responsibilities, I'm no longer a fan of *"through the roof daily expectations."* As I weighed the pros and cons of my situation, I could barely disguise the heaviness I felt pressing against my chest. Generally speaking, when it comes down to explaining, understanding or altering the nature of things, I normally don't mind being the one sitting in the front seat. But this ride is different; it's an onslaught of "ifs." It even has the authority to ride along on one or two incoherent retirement scripts that now place me squarely in the back seat.

When the new day dawned, I saw daylight come escorted by a mixture of more inaccurate public perceptions about retirement and the baby boomers' positioning. What was all this rigmarole that incorrectly called baby boomers "the mollycoddled generation?" Throwing my head back as if to discount my frustration, I couldn't begin to comprehend the reason why that label was affixed to my generation of hard-working people. Then I realized that, in general, millennial believe boomers are the last generation able to collect a decent annuity because, at present, we can still harvest the benefits of the present provincial and federal welfare system.

To my knowledge, this propaganda of falsehood opens the door to serious finger- pointing disputes. It is common knowledge that today, government data has brought to light the fact that Canada has the highest paid public-sector workers in the world. Raising my eyebrows in astonishment at what I just learned, I ask myself this question: Isn't it true this entire monetary reward program has been achieved through vigorous union negotiations? The answer to my own question is: yes, but, what these negotiators neglected to keep in mind is the real reason why some hundred years ago unions were established in the first place. The untold truth is that today, unions have created a labour force that works far less for a lot more money. I don't think that's what Aristotle meant when he said: "Pleasure in the job puts perfection in the work." In addition, some select groups are so privileged they receive extra benefit compensations. Isn't this a slap in the face to the hard- working citizens in the private sector who believe in an honest day's work? I have no patience or sympathy for this lopsided predicament.

It's nearly impossible to digest the makings of this sore topic as more and more government financials carrying huge deficits are made available. Archived regime records tell us how countless millions of dollars have been drawn from the government pension plan that was, and still is, funded by members' dues. It appears that there are large sums of money spent on public sector unions, the same interest groups that are rarely ever studied, questioned, or audited. This doesn't sound like leadership transparency to me. In essence, I would rate this scenario more along the lines of "a botched entitlement mess."

Is it plausible that these missteps are allowed to happen because the majority of Canadian workers are employed by unionized private sectors? Do we know how much of the fat contributions of approximately forty billion dollars annually are selectively used to fund politics, lobbyists, and high-ranking government employee pensions? Without slamming the door on these absurdities, I would recommend that the infrastructure of these top 8 – 10 percent public sector income earners abstain from being so self-righteous and self-indulgent before they throw our economy into a total tail spin. Who is the real mollycoddled society? Whom should we take aim at for the public sector workers' cozy arrangements? Not the boomers!

For subject support and accurate classification, I believe it isn't fair to attribute blame to the boomers for their ability to pass on their gains to their children and grandchildren. I'm also cognizant of the fact that the lifestyle of my generation of reformed citizens was not always full of first-rate fortunes, wide smiles, good health, loud music, and bright sunshine. By supporting and accepting open awareness of our circumstances, we will unanimously agree that more often than not, modifications come with a visible cost attached to them.

The boomers' desire for change, followed by their exploits, is the result of what can be achieved through courage, brave deeds, special efforts, and daily hard and steady work. They voluntarily paid that cost to ensure the future of their children would not be as bleak as the early years of their own lives. This is not molly- coddling. I prefer to call this progression *"the middle class positioning."*

Like many others of my generation, I've been working since the age of fifteen and after all these years, I can't help thinking how I felt on my first day on the job. I recall how excited and scared I was as I stepped into the department store and headed for the supervisor's office to announce my arrival. Today, that memory remains tender and alive, but, it's a reminder of something that happened so long ago. That gentle memory marked the beginning of my working career, whereas now, I'm getting closer to the end of my career. I'm now approaching a demarcation line of a dissimilar meaning. Once again, I feel worried and wound-up as I face my exit from the work force. It's bizarre to think that more than a hundred years ago, the retirement phenomenon now leaving me stressed was a non- existent chapter in senior citizens' lives. In those days, people were expected to work till they could no longer do so; otherwise, their family members would become the responsible party for their livelihood and well being. History has left us many anecdotes that make reference to a number of cases where things did not work out well in that type of setting. This held especially true for the population who lived in the low-income bracket.

In view of ongoing age dilemmas and ethical predicaments, it took the German Chancellor Otto Von Bismark, to finally declare that any citizen of age seventy or older should be entitled to receive a pension, thereby alleviating undue family hardships. Of course, in those days most people lived an average of sixty to sixty-five years. In 1916, Germany therefore lowered the retirement age to sixty-five. Some government think- tanks with no self-public statements to announce, finally took a decisive step toward society's helpful direction. Such action brought relief to young and old, and scrapped the economic helplessness for the assembly of non- working senior citizens. There was no doubt that the dread of getting old had indeed taken a different turn. A healthier, self-sufficient, and more positive life existence had turned up to retrofit the old conventional ageing perspective. The new attitude and novel gratitude made the seniors' days a little brighter. In 1927, McKenzie King, the Canadian Liberal leader, introduced the Old Age Pension Act in

Canada. This was complemented by a pension-income supplement to ensure no senior citizen was living below the poverty line. Then, in 1985, Brian Mulroney of the Canadian Conservative Party arrived full of flamboyancy and busting at the seams with what he thought was a smart budgetary move and tried to de- index the pension benefits. Luckily, his lack of common sense was met with tough protests. The public's voice rang out like loud sirens, and he quickly changed his mind. No further senseless discussions were held after that incendiary encounter.

Shortly after 1985, the United States also saw fit to adopt a similar social security program. A retirement hiatus was awoken. The American senior citizens' legitimate financial assistance program was finally made available to those of age sixty-five and older. The old-age pension was designed to be an entitlement for everyone's well being regardless of income category. A victorious legislative achievement had unmistakably won the hearts of seniors.

Today, this capricious phase takes our personal life to a new level whether the up-and-coming retirees are ready for it or not. For some seniors, retirement means never having to get up early in the morning and go to work again. For others, it means they can leave their present job and start anew in a different and less demanding field. For the well to-do, retirement can denote no longer worrying about making money. As a substitute for work, they can spend as much time as they want playing golf or enjoying all the leisure activities life has offer. Life has something to offer to each one of us when we reach retirement.

Before the next year arrives, my test --- or better still, my goal is to determine what appeals most to me and how

I can think about my senior years with enthusiasm. Perhaps the extra free time I'll have at my disposal can be used to muse over past imperfections and see how the lessons learned from those experiences have served me in the years thereafter. It may even be true that those same frailties coached me to be more forgiving and considerate of other people's similar mistakes whether of a personal or business nature. In the end, the most important message I drew from my mistakes is that sooner or later we all make blunders.

For the first time in a number of years, I didn't need an editorial page to report that modesty is a product of humility, and it undeniably beats arrogance.

Although adaptation and diversification are essential qualities for humans' fundamental survival and emotional endorsement, I, and likely other ageing citizens, may need an extension of time to ultimately come to terms with the unfamiliar withdrawal from work.

As far as I can tell, whining about something we have no control over has never provided sensible solutions for anything or for anyone at any time. The truth is, I should not be feeling like a lone player in the game of age and uncertainties. Whether we like to admit it or not, most of us tend to experience tiny tinkling sensations in our stomach when we begin to absorb the significance of retirement. In the course of accepting this new actuality, the more sensitive individuals might run the risk of having self-induced nausea overtaking their more unbridled personal qualities. If I find myself in this predicament, I customarily turn to laughter as a means of diminishing any dramatic effects. I'm also known to crack a false smile when touched by a cascade of bitter reservations in order to create the expectation that things will eventually turn out all right.

One attention-grabbing action is for me to engage in several mild-mannered investigations for the purpose of gathering viable testimonials from previous retirees' experiences. It would stand to reason that logic would give voice to the newly discovered answers, revealing the tangible benefits of making a well- informed transfer to an impending new life. Those with the foresight to plan ahead should thoroughly re-assess their prearranged retirement package. The next step requires moving forward with ample caution to avoid the hazard of jumping ahead with yesterday's ideas and principles. All too frequently I remind myself not to forge ahead with undisciplined thoughts; otherwise, I may risk tripping and falling on unsafe ground. I believe it's vital not to become paranoid, but it's also fine to hold-out with tact and prudence through a complex situation such as the planning for a sound retirement strategy. Benjamin Franklin said: "By failing to prepare, you are preparing to fail."

It's a tiny but significant point to accept this risk in order to score points for ourselves at this stage of life's game. We must press on without foolish irritability or else we'll needlessly place ourselves in fate's precarious spins and twists. Irritability is neither a sensible nor a recommended path to follow. It can bring us to a state of personal aggravation and frustration resulting in serious grouchiness. When taunted by doubt, we must keep in mind that it's never easy to take the lead in confronting difficult or challenging matters. Seeking an edge means leading, and to lead means not being afraid of taking a chance. The courage to take a chance puts us in a leadership role. Therefore, we must not allow ill-defined trigger points to rob us of our human dexterity and connect us to adversarial consequences. Instead, we must play the game as intended: on a grand gradation and with fingers crossed for an outcome of happy alternatives.

I spend hours theorizing how my plans for retirement need to discard any notion of recklessness. The fear of making a mistake that could cause me to reach the end result with an empty feeling leaves me totally worried. When I stepped back, I felt stressed, dumbfounded, and at a loss for words. Trying to break away from mental tension, I realized I was without charge for any renewed thoughts. Exactly where did I fit in? Why could I not do my best thinking out-loud? What was I worried about?

Why did I feel a lump in my throat every time the word *"retirement"* entered the room?

My thoughts scrambled for a chance to be heard instead of being pushed away to take refuge in a secreted echo-chamber. One would think any reasonable person could easily make expedient decisions based on subject data and the benefits of self-acquired knowledge. But not me! I didn't even have a rough sketch of a promising exit plan in place yet. It's always easier to sit back and take mental notice of things, but what is difficult is to get up and act with creativity.

Until now, I had been of the opinion that such planning was only critical of other people's time frame. Boy, have I been a fool. Sighing deeply, and in no mood for pity, I closed my eyes and immediately saw the word "retirement" morphing into resentment.

WHEN IS THE RIGHT TIME?

- When we see the sand in the hourglass start to shift to the other side.
- When our conversations start with "When I was younger…."
- When we lose sight of who we are today.
- When we allow ourselves to become frustrated as soon as someone says anything that offends us.
- When arthritic pain and aches begin to pay us daily visits.
- When new technology boggles our minds.
- When we allow the future to dominate our fears.
- When we begin to entertain the attraction of living with our children.
- When we become a little too complacent and start dropping or losing interest in our hobbies.
- When we are made aware that people around us prefer we talk less about our past and be more interested in listening to their story instead.
- When we start to question our ability to hold on to our independence.
- When we worry about falling down because it's too hard to get back up.
- When we add prunes and laxatives to the grocery list.

How could this be the right time to think about turning to a new page in my life? I have so much more to do and so many projects to complete. Is this transitional period one of those grey areas that always falls short of leaning toward the white or weighing heavily toward the black area?

Cutting to the chase one afternoon, I came clean with the scenario that, at times, when at home after work, I inadvertently answer the phone with a business greeting instead of the customary hello. Do I always have work on my mind? Perhaps I've contracted *workitis* in my lengthy carrier. That might explain why I'm now stuck at a non-starter position in terms of my no-nonsense exit plan. Is it time to call on strategic thinking to square off this equation? Is it practical to think fast about this intricate situation, or is it wiser to consider further and hope to achieve a well thought-out solution? These questions were spewing out wrathfully and without polish.

From everything I've already heard about retirement planning, I need to keep digging to find some form of resolution. The hope to find an immediate answer seems to be an abortive exercise. To me, coming up with a quick response does not equal arriving at a smart or a convincing resolution. This unavoidable streak of life mystery, which happens when we reach a ripe retirement age, is now teasing my wits to bring me face to face with one of life's new and eccentric kicks. There was no holding back in confessing that I'm clearly not ready to deal with this particular chapter today or any time soon. All I know is that if I press the issue any further today, my hopes for a grand comeback will be thrown away like a contemptible thought. When in doubt, do nothing.

More days passed and somehow I did very well at re-arranging and managing my composure, almost to the point of making my quandary seem like someone else's shadow. I effectively skirted the nagging retirement question for another interim period. Then, I did what I often do when

I'm not sure of what to do: I moved forward by doing my most excellent work both at the office and in my personal life. My befuddled mind was not committing to anything on this calendar day.

Coming into a mean hiccup situation at the office the following week, those irritating and provoking thoughts of retirement resurfaced. Like a bolt of lightning, the stance on retirement planning came at me with a vengeance. But I was not running away from any new business endurance tests nor was I prepared to let another short-lived publicity stunt convince me to make a tentative deal with retirement.

I have faced and experienced a number of malevolent circumstances in the past two and a half decades as chief operator of a service business, so I was no stranger to another temporary block in productivity. This was merely an inconvenient waste of time brought on by a conniving customer who preferred to uselessly lobby against a reasonably balanced work form. As far as I could determine, the episode did not qualify as one of paramount upheaval, nor did it appear as a particularly hard one to solve.

With wholehearted admiration for the conflict resolution etiquette shown by my management staff, I proudly watched them manage the situation with total control and self-assurance. They expertly resolved the issue without taking in too much gaffe. In a few words, the situation clearly highlighted the genuine significance of practicing solid business principles and excellent work ethics. The depth of payback from our monthly operational exchanges on the topic of problem- solving techniques proved exceptionally valuable in this instance, and the authentic results came afloat like a real winner. As if taken by storm, I remembered that a long time ago, a wise person told me that business does not spare anyone from daily maelstroms nor does it protect any person from the potential of coming across difficult situations. Nothing will distinguish you as a business champion simply because you consider yourself smart when things come easy or when you successfully manage to swerve away unscathed from an impending struggle. In business, creative problem- solving is an indispensable skill. I'm referring to the kind of skill that may or may not be something learned in an MBA program. There is also the probability that if this deftness were, in fact, taught as part of the curriculum, the student may have been absent on that day.

As a form of work habit, I often take the liberty of outlining three easy problem-solving steps to my management staff. I give emphasis to my theory that not much will remain ablaze if we follow these three simple techniques:

- First, identify the problem and its starting point.
- Second, explain it in its most uncomplicated form and identify your options.
  Always have more than one option available.
- Third, conduct a win-lose analysis so you can classify the most likely solution that will benefit your company.

This was definitely one of the days I felt glad to have met this sensible person and equally pleased to have heeded his wisdom. In my chosen lifestyle, his shrewd words became my guide and, with that, I learned to get through each work day in a watchful fashion. In turn, this practice has helped make each of my days a new adventure. The ability to practice and benefit from what you learned can only come alive with the occasion to put your knowledge to the test. Napoleon Bonaparte said: "Ability is nothing without opportunity."

But here are more difficult questions: Am I drawn to the erratic business world? Am I looking at opportunity as something dressed in a suit posturing as work? I don't know, but maybe that's enough speculating for now. It all seems momentous and strange to me, but after a few of my "one person" roundtable talks, I still can't quite put my finger on the pulse. I'm talking about my own pulse - that of a middle aged woman who for many years has thrived by investing her valuable time and energy in a fast-paced business environment. I even dared run through some of my days on nervous strength to ensure the proposed targets were met and not swallowed by inattentiveness. Depth of knowledge and systematic competencies are vital business measures that have branded the insignia of common sense for me and my management staff. I'm convinced that a company's overall performance evaluation can be directly linked to each individual's deeds, goals, skills and dedication. It may sound simple, but in all reasonableness, it's a tough task to arrive at work every day with the sole objective of pushing the bottom-line needle to a new height.

My so-called "high-flying strategy" is composed of the following points: If there is a reasonable goal that can be measured and evaluated, it can also be achieved. But, as the years run by, and time weighs down on us, there comes a day in everyone's life when we have to bridge the gap between our spot in the fast lane of the industrial sphere and walking at a slower pace on the road of leisure. Most reform-minded business people do not waste useful time hesitating then rushing to figure out who might best fill their shoes when they outgrow them. They do not shy away from scrutinizing how best to transfer their accumulated industry knowledge to the new cohorts. Unlike most, I was no doubt acting a little bashful and a bit heavy-handed with the new selection. After many years in the work force, now may well be a good time for me to take a long look at the bigger picture and reflect on giving the new generation opportunities in my business.

This is not a comic story; I'm advancing toward the foothills of a new phase in my life. Still, I'm far from being psychologically ready to make any sound decisions about retirement. I'm slowly coming to the realization that we don't need to be tough or smart to survive, but we need to be receptive to change.

As one day ended and a new one dawned, I continued to ask myself these questions: Where can I find the proper point of reference that indicates the beginning of one's new crossing and the end of another? Who is best qualified to help me make this decision? I really needed to figure this out soon. Maybe in the summer, or possibly the fall would be a better time to bring these distinctive elements of my life together. Perhaps at that time, I can make an effort to wrap them up satisfactorily; as soon as I figured out what my satisfactory fit was made of. I was becoming quite efficient at deferring the inevitable. And during that interlude, I was able to push away all thoughts and worries of what repercussions my decision could bring to light. I felt a headache coming on. I am not an impulsively reactionary person, nor have I ever been scared to make a difficult business decision, but the thought of retirement left me standing motionless, speechless, and anesthetized. My facial expressions kept bouncing from contempt to restlessness, and I felt as much intrigued as I was flabbergasted by this concept. At that moment, the slightest breeze could have knocked me off my feet and I wouldn't have felt a thing. A strange but novel reality of an up-to-the- minute narrative was budding in my space.

A new window of unusual opportunities was opening for me --- neither a day too soon or too late. There must be more than one choice available to mature adults when we reach this special stage in our lives. If questions and answers typically walk in parallel lines, then by engaging in a sizeable research-and- study developmental project, I should hit upon a better understanding of the parameters of this topic.

In the days that followed, I pressed on without losing myself in more self-imposed cynicism. Searching through whatever statistical records I could find, I uncovered an outline of what my predecessors and other people within my age group were up to. I was now more determined than ever to delve into this study with a promise and strength of mind to find the correct formula. The initial facts divulged by this exposé were hard to digest, but I was not about to be deterred from my mission. These skilled pollsters pulled no punches when it came to presenting a well framed illustration meant to depict our full cycle of life. My nerves were jolted that day as I continued to read through a compilation of retirement schematics. I found that the legitimacy of the content had no sense of humor and the grandeur of its report sent shockwaves through my system.

For the most part, the chronicled particulars indicated that a sizeable number of baby boomers choose semi-retirement while most others prefer full retirement. It also pointed out that a good number of bona-fide chief executive officers from large organization are more inclined to prefer early retirement, typically averaging age fifty-five. Characteristically speaking, those positions are so exhausting and full of sky-scraping expectations that the person risks running out of steam after a number of years at the pinnacle of their career. The end result is that these exceptional performers eventually lose the joy of forever having to keep up with that territorial aggressiveness. A top executive position can be very rewarding and uplifting, but the perils that accompany the benefits oftentimes defy logic and infringe on their personal wellness. A proficient executive's job is driven by total commitment, above-average vision and heightened affirmative performance in growth and originality whether they face harsh economic times or not.

It must be a forlorn and downhearted atmosphere up there and it can't be a pleasant spot to uphold for a long period of time. Perhaps these executives have the necessary courage and endurance level to outdo the loneliness that awaits them in their rarified world. It comes as no surprise that after a number of years at such fine-tuned speed, the idea of spending more quality time with their family becomes an inviting and fulfilling substitute. However, for some chief executive officers, after a few months of rest from a fierce pace, they are ready to engage in a semi-business mission or become part-time mentors to smaller entrepreneurs. To their credit, every now and then, their services are offered free of charge at community centres or through local retiree-mentor programs and small business organizations. This alternative represents a win-win situation for both parties; one side gains knowledge and guidance while the other side gains gratitude, a boost to their self-worth, and integrity preservation.

In other general facets, sixty-five seemed to be a popular age to change course. However, in a number of instances, individuals may be encouraged to leave their posts earlier by being offered a healthy departing package once they reach the qualifying number factor. I'm personally acquainted with people who for years devoted all their energy to proficiently carrying out their duties in the position of middle or senior management then opting to accept a parting package at age fifty-five. Many early retirees have eventually spoken out about the reason they came to accept the wind-up arrangement with their employer. Their decision was not due to the financial enticement or the company's restructuring course of action. Given how my contemporaries and I have engaged in several conversational exchanges in reference to retired life, I'm increasingly convinced my friends have been driven to that finale strictly by the desire to disentangle themselves from poorly managed conglomerates continuously missing the operational mark. These unqualified geniuses fruitlessly outsource what is readily available within, mismanage the company's finances by running a ludicrous deficit, and constantly assign blame to middle or senior management by accusing them of not working smart or fast enough.

The so-called "executives" who sit at the top of such bungled establishments have successfully managed to secure themselves a large remuneration but are not necessarily the ones who understand or ever figure out what the front-line staff's responsibilities are worth. They are unmoved by the work load assigned to middle management and frequently turn a blind eye to the number of employees pressed to go on stress leave. It is worrisome to be aware of these adversities and yet have no say about the unprofessional workings of phony executives. These frauds successfully manage to create an agenda for themselves that is made up of coming to their office in the morning, asking their assistant to bring them coffee, reading a few reports, shooting the proverbial breeze with their subordinates, and slipping out at rapid speed to join their peers for more gratifying social activities.

On the day that gossip, insinuations, and wild speculation show an unfavourable financial bottom line, they expertly pick a scapegoat on which to unload their two-pronged bit of malice. Essentially, the fact that their dismal actions cause real life penalties to hard-working people does not seem to be of any concern to them. One learns very fast how these imposter executives are experts at dishing out praise or sourness to two different sides at the same time. Their actions carry no shame as long as their knee-jerking scheme is kept intact. In my opinion, this miscalculated displacement of competent resources is not a mystery. It is basically a prime example of what happens when the top executives become wrapped up in entitlement that they get blindsided by a disconnect with the above-board members of their production team. Their speeches sometimes reek of foolishness, their empty words lack reference to the organization's order of business and the enterprise's real mission. Evaluations of productivity, financial status, and skillfully calculated projections simply become non-energizers of their daily campaign. When caught in the mesh of such unprofessional calamity, the employees who can afford it tend to lean toward early retirement and gladly accept a financial package once the offer is made. Those who accept this choice, call the move a step toward personal and professional independence. Additionally, they consider this to be a double step away from the bosses who excel in deceptive work practices and who go through life without a conscience.

These unprofessional chief executive officers place themselves in a jurisdiction full of cushy entitlements without any remorse or shame for their malfeasance. Since these situations usually carry enough blame to go around, it's safe to say the organizations that employ these CEOs are also at fault for allowing such failures in management style. In cases like these, comprehensive reforms for workplace civility would be grandstanding but would surely knock the socks off the fake executives.

TECHNOLOGY IS TO BLAME

Another well-known causative factor and clear-cut culpable trespasser that's here to encourage an early departure from the work place is the accelerated technological progress. This demanding intruder has reached unprecedented levels of complexity and is a little unfriendly toward an ageing demographic.

Technology does not take into consideration that the brain of people over the age of fifty-five works more slowly if only because it is already overloaded with information gathered from past decades and has been stored away. It must be for this reason senior citizens frequently experience moments of memory loss. There is an old fable about an elderly doctor practicing medicine part- time, and in the course of the day, he makes a house call to see a patient suffering from bronchitis. Proceeding with the examination, he reaches in his medical pouch for a thermometer but pulls out a tongue depressor instead. He looks at the instrument in his hand. "Oh no," he says. "I must have left my thermometer in the previous patient's anal passage."

The use of computers and the internet have taken positions of great speed and have inadvertently, or selectively, created a noticeable distance between the older and the newer generation. Technology has squarely defined itself as a necessary asset for today's culture. We have moved on from the generation of the Great Depression, Baby Boomers, and Generation X, and have now arrived at the "texting generation." Clearly, texting or emailing is the creative alternative that has become the first means of communication and seriously outranks making a phone call. It's the preferred method of communication because it is expedient, economical, and bypasses having to speak with anyone face-to-face. Technology is here to stay even if some of us believe it has created a generational divide when it comes to communication skills. I surmise it's true that the boomer generation still likes to write letters and speak to people in person or over the phone, while the younger generation is proficient at using more updated tools like iPhones, Skype, tablets, computers and whatever else the technological market makes available to them. Unlike most mature adults, the millennials have no issue carrying on a relationship with someone they met on-line and subsequently discover they have things in common. Their interaction is kept alive via Facebook, LinkedIn, Twitter or suchlike carriers they may be connected to. Dissimilar to millennials, I still consider writing the best and most efficient method of enhancing the ability to interact or liaise properly. Also, having a real phone conversation with a person gives me the advantage of expression and permits an identification of emotions. To me, this thumps the unvarying beep-beep emitted from electronic keyboards.

In a last-ditch attempt to ride out my unsettling chaos, I switched my attention back to my colleagues' new-found daily activities once their retirement freedom took place.

I began to make my way downstairs for no apparent reason. All the way down, I gripped the railing as if I needed a firm grip on any and all potential avoidance of my vacillating retirement thoughts. In my constant struggle to get to the brass roots of this issue and figure out how and when to draw the most appropriate dividing line between work and leisure time, I felt a surge of relief knowing that, for my colleagues, retirement had broadened their horizons with a fresh sense of being. They had also developed an appreciation for world events, nurtured many new acquaintances, joined recreational activities, engaged in travel several times a year, spent some of their free time doing volunteer work, and opened a new screen for family and neighbourhood commitments.

Still, this leisurely interlude is not a permanent deal that will see them through to the rest of their mature life. After two years of living this renewed life style, their astonishing progress did not cancel- out my prediction they would contemplate part-time employment. Although this type of post-retirement progression may not hold true for everyone who retires early, it certainly prompts me to continue with more investigation and reflection. I went on with more study about my retirement and the possible immediate and long-term effects it might have on me. One should not ignore loose-ends or logistical points when making a statement about the impact of a new experience. With thought after thought dominating my psyche, it was best to arrive at a resolution free of reservation and without eroding the confidence of my decision to switch track only at the right time and for the right reason.

The decisive moment to look at the platform I refer to as a "bumpy, weird, and wonderful experience" was now standing in front of me with its fixed stare determined to study my every twitch. That was the instant indecision took the lead and proposed I laugh this off, as things could be worse. But then caution jumped in like a designated chaperone. It inflicted enough fear to make me think that if I got into high spirits and laughed at my situation, things might become visibly worse. Damn the retirement decision-making process! This is a saga of never-ending regurgitating questions and apprehensions.

With a lot of question-marks emanating from unresolved duality, the slightest sign of a smile jumped off my face. Struggling with the temptation to break down the retirement message to a few flippant words, I came to the conclusion my objective faced an absence of retirement touch-points. Once again, a wise notion flashed by my ears, saying: "When in doubt - do nothing." For a while, I felt rescued and did just that - nothing. When the dust settled, I turned my new focus to the chart that lay motionless before me.

Surprisingly, the concise breakdown of details was very enlightening. The particulars pointed out that at the present rate of retirement; it is feasible that by the year twenty-twenty we could face the lurking risk of losing a significant number of talents. The industrial zones stand to suffer a shortage of people with proven experience and unmatched skills as large numbers of seasoned business professionals make their exit from the work force. Such mass exoduses would be the calling card for the younger generation to set in motion a long courtship with the industrial and commercial sectors to ensure the world does not become a sphere desolate of intellect.

At one point, I almost felt like saying, "who's got time to read this crap?" Instead, I prodded myself to take a look through the telescope of the future. New ideas swarmed me as soon as I began to envision an onslaught of business challenges being downloaded onto the younger generation, who may or may not be ready for such a life changing experience. I could picture the puzzled look on their faces once they decide to cross through the exotic regions of the industrial world. It will be interesting to watch them zero-in and push far beyond the present business nucleus with the aim of keeping the occupational locomotive moving forward and moving fast. There is one thing that isn't clear to me yet; will any of my business experience add valuable financial or operational curves for young entrants? Then again, I could presume they're in harmony with the wise words spoken by Bill Bradley: "Ambition is the path to success. Persistence is the vehicle you arrive in." Or, perhaps they've heard Vidal Sasson's message: "The only place success comes before work is in the dictionary."

I've been drawing reassurance and knowledge from those shrewd words for many years. Time after time, feeling backed by the strength of those proverbs, I ventured forward never taking a step back or shying away from harsh conditions that got in my way. Similarly, I seldom considered halting my business progression when the operation experienced difficulties reaching a middle-ground resolution. Holding my line at work and doing my finest at whatever I was engaged in was my way of making myself and my team capable of generating positive bottom-line results. On the other hand, I don't recall a single time when I dared dismiss the concept that doing your best doesn't always translate into a winning strategy nor does it guarantee you a successful undertaking.

I've been through numerous occasions when, along with my staff, I managed to stifle a negative situation simply by applying common sense. We've always taken our wins without being brash. We've taken our losses with our heads held high, proud of our effort, and walked away with written notes to learn from.

My methodology is to basically wear down the people who want to challenge a non-arguable business point. Sometimes, my operating style projects the sentiment that it's more advantageous, if not sagacious, to avert any provocation with the potential to make me look less of a pro and more like a business fool. I am not a fan of fools.

Habitually, I tend to do well when I need to turn a downbeat situation to my benefit by indirectly making the other party assume responsibility for the unnecessary bickering. My employees see this as a class-act they love to watch and learn from. I take some comfort knowing that every now and again I actually complete off-putting encounters with such gusto that I irritate the daylights out of the rival characters. For anyone who might be interested in my formula, here is my rule of thumb:

A) Think and have a plan in place before you tackle a given situation.
B) Facts are hard to dispute.
C) Money cannot buy or sell common sense to anyone.

While more busy months go by and no spark for an exit plan is ignited, I keep going with my demanding routine. One day, as I sat working at my file-covered desk, I paused to take a sip of espresso coffee, and I began to imagine a variant workplace scenario. If all went according to some plan, in the not-so-distant future, there would be sweat beads running down Generation Y's faces as they take a crack at managing the might of our volatile commercial and industrial repute. In truth, I found this evolution both worrisome and intriguing. The first questions to flood my mind were: Would they be frightened, or would they be ready to meet the industry's demands with fairness and integrity?

Will the young trainees who come to the business forefront aspiring to become full-fledged business entrepreneurs fold in half?

Will they be subjected to grueling sensations similar to what people get when they wound up facing Chuck Norris in an unpleasant situation?

In Chuck's presence, even the toilet will flush away by itself if he sneezes loudly. With his superior martial-arts proficiency, Chuck Norris never loses. But entrepreneurship is not as well protected or insulated from any financial tragedy, even with the presence of sound operational skill and organizational expertise.

In the business world, there are definite possibilities for harsh encounters with poor talent and an abundance of sluggish productive days. Odd as it may seem, when faced with coldhearted fiscal losses, even the seasoned operators who have been in business for a number of years can only suck in their breath and wish they had chosen a different career. In that case, occasion makes available a perfect trade-off not only by suggesting it, but by asserting that retirement really is the ideal alternative for them.

I'm still active at work every day of the week, and I have more questions than answers about my upcoming retirement. The commitment to make my transitioning process appear seamless got me looking back at the two young men who on more than one occasion expressed the desire to take over the reins when I was ready to step down, or slow down. Are these individuals charged with sufficient creative energy, and are they ready to carry out varied business plans? I now had more questions that deserved clear and concise answers, but, who could I pose the next three questions to?

#1 Are they ready to determine if a potential new hire claiming to be a "fast learner" could possibly mean they have never had any previous training or experience in this field?

#2 Are they savvy enough to figure out what the applicants looking for service positions mean when they say they have a "consistent driving record?" Will they pick up that it could mean they often disobey the speed limit but have not been caught yet?

#3 Will they see through a questionable answer given by potential applicants seeking sales positions who say "they have made many contacts?" Will they know that it could mean they have made many unsuccessful calls over the phone?

Putting it bluntly, I felt sandwiched between the need to take frequent deep breaths and the call to reconcile the yearning for a clear understanding of where my two companies' future was headed. Most specifically, I wanted to be on the level with my expectations of what my future ought to look like. In my mind, I wondered if, in the history of the world, anyone had ever been successful at mitigating a future with little or no risks to themselves and for skirting the anguish of leaving their business behind. If they did try, did they fear for worst as they went through the process? Would all hell break lose if they failed?

I felt like a rookie trying to get a handle on an infrastructure that was put together for the sole reason of making life more scattergun than strategic. To top it off, I was attempting to do this while concealing the fear in my eyes. Figuratively speaking, this cumbersome encounter with a new reality turned out to be the spark that redirected my attention to the cognitive data I had gathered not so long ago regarding the boomers' exit from the work-force. This informal retirement bulletin acted as a tutor that mentored the interest of anyone who had a stake in it. Its purpose was to bring awareness of the facts. There are a lot of unknowns about my future. Each day seems to come with a different essence, and today, the realization that life is a delicate endowment, and longevity is not to be taken for granted, sent shockwaves through my spine. But I was secure where I was, and frankly, at this age I'm not a big risk taker.

THE ALTERNATIVES

Emotions of Retirement

The turn-of-the-year as well as world events addressing retirement particulars are enough to give me goosebumps. In my recent travel to Japan, I was surprised to learn that in the last twenty years, Japan has been facing slower economic growth since the boomers decamped. Europe is undergoing comparable economic conditions and is close to catching up to Japan. Canada is similarly starting to experience a chain reaction of slower growth, weaker investments, and increased budget demands due to health-care costs, augmented pension payments, and other expenses to ensure the well being of the ageing population. As I read more retirement bulletins, my eyes surely must have seen a neon sign warning me against the danger of stepping into a bottomless cavity of retirement statistics overload. This quantitative data called for a momentary hiatus so that I could examine and absorb the meaning and implications reported by this unprejudiced presentation of details.

Setting my disparagement aside, I settled down and accepted, with some reservation, the results gathered and presented by the expert fact-finders and record-keepers of the aging society. I continued to read and soak up more helpful retirement information. Maybe I was involuntarily looking for flaws in the existing records. Or maybe I was simply toying with the facts. These statistics disclosed that women in their late fifties or early sixties (my circle of populace) tend to live to the age of eighty-four. No kidding! By the genius of simple math, I figured I had quite a few years to go yet. So why retire now? What will I do with all that free time? How will I stimulate my brain?

Holy cow, why does transitioning have to be such a hard negotiator?

The scariest quandary of all: Was I in danger of being discounted or even becoming accustomed to feeling depressed after a few months of not having to deal with the daily stresses of work? I was not yet ready or willing to entertain the possibility of an uneventful life style. How do you face this unease of separating yourself from what you worked so hard to establish and maintain for many years? How do you conquer the ability to underscore the anxiety that comes with it? There is no debating the fact that for now, my present structure continues to suite me fine. I have good reason to beat the alarm clock in the morning. Being the person in charge and the one fully responsible for the successful operation of two service-oriented companies and a serious number of employees is hard, challenging, and, sometimes nerve- wrecking. But all this is what keeps me physically and mentally active and unquestionably occupied.

So far, most of my attempts to productively referee a variety of monologues regarding my retirement state-of-affairs have not rewarded me with a winning case. I feel stressed admitting I haven't been successful in bringing together any alluring thoughts about the imminent changeover. However, I think I have a convincing argument when I say that my past years of devotion and of working like a suspension bridge-builder among employees, suppliers, and customers alike amounts to work longevity. What a darned life process this is!

Now that I've made progress mastering my life's mission, and my children are grown up and self- sufficient,

I'm facing the unsought natal regulator trying to rob me of more valuable occasions. This nameless age watchdog arrives with the boldness to impose distinct changes to people's itinerary: retirement. Seriously? No wonder my emotions are doing summersaults. I cannot believe or even pretend to accept either the tone or the cheek of this phenomenon.

Today, I'm still living a productive life, but subconsciously, I think I agree that a little less stress would be in my best interest. This holds especially true when electronic technology demands I stay tuned with, and on top of, the new information age. While not making it too apparent, I do not conceal the fact that the Twitter fascination and the internet's communication techniques are not my close friends. My logic doesn't begin to filter the value of such excessive use of either Twitter or the internet. People who are thoroughly engrossed in this type of communication give me the impression they may not be comfortable at personal discourse. Many of them readily and continuously offer plenty of that confirmation. If you give someone a Twitter account, they'll get so engrossed in it that there is a good chance they'll even forget to eat their meals. There is a general belief that if you ask a Twitter user what life means to them, they'll answer by asking where they can download that app from.

The other dispiriting factor I cannot wrap my head around are the constant "*déjà whoops*" officiated by government legislators who, without proper external input from business owners, or human resource professionals, implement more and more redundant labour rules and policies for businesses to abide by. This by no means improves workplace cultures, attitudes or standards. It only adds up to more of the same directives many business owners have already put in practice by using simpler and more cost-effective resolutions. When all is said and done, the only things the misinformed legislators manage to accomplish are more wasted production time and less work being done.

On many occasions, poor use of the human resource managers' talents results in corporations being forced to know more about the shenanigans that go on in government offices than about the employees who work for their company. I admit that I'm beginning to get frustrated and tired of dealing with this intrusive incompetence day in and day out. After so many years of putting up with valueless governmental blunders, the onset of a different way of living my days to come elicits a huge grin. A lighter burden could really be a connecting pass to a temporary resolution for my open question: "Should I or shouldn't I retire yet?" Is this simply an issue of time? Am I overdramatizing the retirement point?

Having been dominated by these questions for so long, I'm leaning toward the option to modify my current role by either restructuring or downsizing. Both are obtainable alternatives and either one would be a fine substitute for full retirement. Finally, I'm reaching the junction point of time-recognition and concrete affirmation for a step-aside date. I can now begin my transition in scaling back even though I keep claiming I have a lot of work to do yet. Pushing to stay the course, I turn down the idea to keep extending my business responsibilities if only to make sure things would keep running smoothly.

My senior staff and I held a number of serious talks about grooming the two intended successors within the organization to ensure they keep the business engine running without the need to fasten their seatbelts. It wouldn't be long before I deal with this conversion in a fittingly holistic manner regardless of the size of the company's growth. Pondering what my future days may look like, I attempted to sneak a preview of where life may lead me. I was engulfed in my thoughts when a bizarre sense of mixed emotions told me to snap out of it. Eventually, I obeyed.

In the stillness of the evening, I wondered if leaving your business might be like the end of a session where a hailstorm of talks can make things seem more or less all right. Or, could this be more like a dual process that marks both the end and the beginning of something larger and utterly superior to anything I have ever known before. Then again, I admit at this point that I'm a few steps closer to the end of my career and not a few steps into my career.

Beyond any other issue, I pulled myself together, adjusted my cloudy focus, and let this situation play out with constructive conformity. I understood that my goal was to make sure I firmly pass on the companies to my successors with appropriate forecasts for a sustainable future. Figuring out if my intended successors would be up to the task was, in part, my responsibility, but ultimately, the commitment to keep up with positive results and a healthy balance sheet would be out of my jurisdiction once I was no longer in the picture. It was all up to these two young entrepreneurs to put in view their uncompromising aspirations and business acumen. It would be up to them to show they have big enough shoulders to sustain the company's weight.

Are the two individuals I have in mind the ones who possess a forward vision without the fear of becoming overextended or burned out?

Once again, I catch myself in the same monologue, claiming it was a necessary obligation to make sure I didn't overlook any possible slip-ups, or avoidable blunders. There is no room for errors in this type of business calculus. I readily acknowledge there is good talent out there geared up for an opportunity to unchain strategic business insights and prove they are ready to make a difference. However, let's just say that if the last twenty-seven plus years taught me anything, it's this: To know something and theorize about it is grand, but, being able to apply that knowledge and accept its results, whatever they may be, requires a certain amount of nobility in your character.

It appears that very soon I'll have some succession planning to delve into. In the days that followed, the soliloquy of preparedness echoed in my mind. Its purpose did not charm me but it encouraged me to take a sober look at what lay ahead. That sullen message might have been telling me I was getting closer to exiting from my business space, or maybe common sense was calling out to declare it was time to harvest what I had sown. Was I floored? Close, but not yet. While soul-searching, I came to the conclusion it wasn't yet time for the retirement train, therefore, I was not about to obsess over it. That was the solemn excuse I constantly leaned on to cover up my procrastination. But as we all know, in order to avoid regret, we're required to make a choice.

The occasion to retract from my low-level interest in this sore subject was now full blown. A dreamlike moment had captivated my attention. A few days later, I returned to my usual character and I began drafting a tentative retirement plan. I promised myself I'd take a reasonable stab at narrowing it down to a well-rounded, wide-ranging package before the potential of missing out on a good plan became a missed opportunity.

In that new brightness, dragging my behind was not the logical or correct answer any longer. I needed to take a chance and hope for the best. If the results didn't measure up to my expectations, or didn't pay off at the end of the journey, I'd have to live with it. In the weeks that followed, I repeated *"holy crap"* at least a million times as I tried to seize the level of personal importance this subject represented. It was a time to think carefully, stay in step with the new revelation, and not waste time on self-pity. Regardless of my reluctance to accept the concept at hand, my new drive urged me to see that this matter outsized the importance of my pride. My transitioning period was indeed happening, and the outcome had to provide for my future's well being. The pinnacle of my retirement lunacy brought the understanding that the years were not trying to invalidate my identity. The occasion was meant only to affirm my sense of being and my worth.

THE EXIT PLAN AND THE REWARD

"Exit planning" presented a dismal, but serious, if not complex, ordeal for me. There was nothing energizing about it. In a gush of mixed thoughts, it came to me that such change would not only include and affect the people arriving at my administrative level; shockingly, it would consist of my *departing from that level. Now what?*

Is it my day of reckoning? If this part were to emulate a one-person train wreck, I'd scream, "This is not my stop!" But, I refrained knowing my outburst would amount only to noise.

Is there a winner strategy I should be referring to or be aware of? I doubt such a thing even exists. Maybe each one of us has the responsibility to do our own calculations and figure out what will work best for us. If you are a business owner, it's wise to have a plan in place rather than to delay the obvious then act astounded and disappointed if the company takes a turn you hadn't envisioned. I didn't want to be caught unprepared by failing to pre-plan or formalize an exit plan in anticipation of that infamous notice. If I fail to plan properly, my new homeward bound days could turn my life into a storyline of nastiness. I could face going to my retirement domicile with an empty wallet and a deflated ego. That would generate a long talk about fractured emotions. Such a collapse of common sense could turn out to be an emotional fiasco of large margins for me. It could even be the root cause of many lamentable "ifs" and bouts of low self-esteem. Where had the confidence-building dynamics I've always believed in disappear to?

A decade ago, I had envisioned the moment of my retirement notice to circulate among my employees like a statement that didn't parrot anything I had ever said before. My message would be heartfelt, simple, and to the point. I would be cautious not to run off at the mouth with unnecessary details about my struggles to come to terms with my semi-retirement adjudication. I most emphatically did not want them to hear the nostalgia in my voice or detect the secret tears circling in my eyes. All I'd comment on would be about my dreams for the upcoming years. I get it - I'm starting to sound like a retirement junkie.

Then, on a whim, I ditched most of my retirement uncertainties and took hold of the reasons for making fundamental changes in my life. The next day, I resolved that aligning one's personal goal as well as their business performance requires knowledge, skill, and expertise especially when dealing with the element of deferring potential tax implications. It became of critical importance to be well aware of my business worth and its market demand before deeming any proposal worthy of a solid and comprehensive package.

I began lining up the relative building blocks that at first seemed simple to assemble, only to find they are a complex progression. I quickly learned that being the original and sole designer of your exit strategy could seriously become a disconcerting and confusing task. I was surprised to find that the longer I sifted through the information, the more amazed I felt at the high yield of options available.

A facilitator or field expert may be just what was needed to help me figure out and define which selection would best suit my application. By embracing that alternative, on the twentieth day of July, I made one last ditch attempt at coming up with a convincing layout before turning the project over to an evaluation expert. The anticipation of my next move brought on an avalanche of scoffs. After a few minutes of nervous tension, I shook my head to avoid bordering on self- pity. Then, talking without expecting anyone to jump in with an answer, I raised this question aloud: Is there such a thing as a happy and satisfied retirement concept out there? A momentary lull is what I finally settled on. I scratched my head trying to figure out how a person remains jovial during this transition without needing long talks with those willing to listen. This is not a decision to be made alone, lightly, or overnight. But how long will it take to get the proper motivation to move forward with the right perspective and a conclusive decision?

My first deliberation was this: The concept of looking forward to retirement feels like an imperfect perception. In the end, I concluded that in the next few days, weeks, or months, I had to do some final negotiating with this emotional carousel. I needed to begin drafting my transition to step down as CEO of my two service companies. The good thing is that I don't have to worry about updating my resume for this impending interview, nor do I need to prove good work ethics to anyone. Retirement has no desire to verify your problem-solving skills or ask you for three references to confirm you as a good candidate. I also know I'm the best expert on my life and I don't have to agonize about receiving a good-quality response from the Human Resources Department. The best part of this process is that the pension boss does not have the authority to dismiss or sequester my application. Another benefit is that it will now be a fitting and appropriate excuse to say that I had a "senior moment" when I forget something. Then again, I don't suppose that retirement shows up empty-handed. It must come with a quantity of paybacks to ease the transition as we shift gear and turn the corner toward this retreat. Of course, having the time to search for discount coupons offers economic advantages, as do senior discounts offered in restaurants and public transportation.

For the many people whose financial situation has managed to arrive at a comfortable level, the freedom of not worrying about having to make mortgage payments is no doubt an added bonus. I would add travel as a good basis for defeating aloneness or dullness. At minimum, travel acts as a temporary arbitrator between not having enough time in a day and what to do with all the free time each day. Knowing that it's not in my DNA to spend my days sitting on a comfortable sofa chair watching soap operas on TV, I was determined to come up with a laudable plan that didn't include too much lazy time. I let my imagination run riotously, thinking about what my new life should look like. I took care not to over-plan for tomorrow and disregard living for today. Without doubt, an exit strategy can work as a confidence builder especially when your contingency plan is designed in your own stylish retirement format. I'm convinced that my newly discovered leisure time will not become the daily norm in my life, nor would it equal doing nothing. It's hardly likely that anyone in their right mind would stick a corny label on the idea of ranking the retirement days as our time to recharge.

In the presence of fair energy and a large container of optimism, any retiree can reach out and feel on top of the world. Once that plateau is reached, they should put into practice a phantom march that stimulates their mental, physical, and emotional balance. It's a definite advantage not to waste valuable time brooding over the times we spent worrying about what we could have done better or the manner in which we dealt with things we had no control over. Sadly, we cannot recover the time, nor can we revisit what we didn't do as well as we might have done had we tried a little harder. We can, however, make the most of what is still to come with the life experiences we now have.

I am finally closing in on my step-aside project fulfillment. After big displays of outward smiles and inward disquiet, my exit plan is almost completed to my liking. Cheers! My plan is no longer spinning in the air, lost in Nowhereland.

In my recent quest to gather facts from diverse retirees' opinions and experiences, I've come away with the understanding that there is no accredited right or wrong exit plan. Many people really do retire happy and live the life they long waited for: slow-paced or doing nothing at all. For me, that selection was discounted without a second thought since I don't much care to operate at speed limits made up of "slow" and "stop." There are those who seem to refuse to admit they've reached a new stage in life and live each day in chaos, trying to relive their past. In their folly, they make an attempt at competing with the younger generation in a futile and absurd effort at proving their worth. A good daily look in the mirror might offer them a little assistance in truth recognition. To my delight, I also learned that many new retirees take pride in swinging the banner of happiness as they explain that growing old beats dying young and the best is yet to come. Their philosophy is to keep as active as your body will allow and stay engaged in such activities as playing a mean game of golf, taking ballroom dancing lessons, joining seniors' social clubs, organizing dinner parties, partaking in Church activities, and doing volunteer work. Those who can afford it, engage in travels to unusual and exotic places around the world. Whether we choose to acknowledge it or not, it may be worth savoring the fact that today we live in a culture that reveres the arts, holds sports in high regard, keeps trying to improve the education system, admires architecture, and takes pleasure in culinary delight among other enchantments. Our present environment has something that makes a difference for each one of us. The globe offers many attractions and adventures that showcase and re-create yesterday's immense beauty while elevating our views to a more advanced technological and astronomical tomorrow. Travel can be described as a visual geography, history, and culinary class combination. My passion for travel has been like a wonderful trick-or-treat transaction, which over the years, has taken me to many splendid places, some of which are illustrated below.

Emotions of Retirement

Helsinki, Finland – Senaatintori Square or Senate Square is located in the centre of Helsinki. The centre is open to many cultural activities. The square has a permanent bronze statue of Tsar Alexander ll. In 1812, Tsar Alexander ll changed the capital of Finland from Turku to Helsinki in order to show the power of the new Russian Regime. December 6 is the celebration of Finland's Independence Day. Photo taken in 2015.

Tallin is the largest city and the capital of Estonia (in the Baltic region). Its city rights were received in 1248. Above is one of the main streets in the centre of the old town. It has many open air shops, restaurants, cafés, souvenir shops and beautiful architecture. During the period from the 14th to the 16th centuries, Tallin became a major trading hub due to its strategic location. Today, Tallin has a population of about 400,000 and is said to be one of the best preserved medieval cities in Europe. Photo taken in 2014

Alexander Nevsky Cathedral in Tallin, Estonia. This Cathedral was designed by Mikhail Preobrazhensky during the period of 1895 to1900 when Estonia was part of the Russian empire. The four Evangelists on the main cupola's arches were painted by the Emperor's court painter, Blaznov. It is believed that the Cathedral was built on the grave of the Estonian hero, Kalev. For many people, that is the explanation of why this building has suffered many structural difficulties. The Alexander Nevsky Cathedral remained closed during the German occupation period. Service was resumed in 1945. Photo taken in 2015.

A typical house in the Stockholm Archipelago. To sail the waters of the Archipelago is to sail over a scattered 60 kilometer radius in the Baltic Sea. Sweden has a population of approximately 10 million people. This number makes it the 90th most densely inhabited country in the world. Photo taken in 2014.

The Quadriga (seen as the goddess of victory) sitting on top of Brandenburg Gate in Berlin portrays the "triumph of peace." In 1806, after Napoleon and his troop invaded Berlin, the Quadriga was transported to Paris. But after Napoleon's defeat in 1814, it was brought back to Brandenburg Gate. Photo taken in 2014

Wrangnell, Alaska. This magnificence sits in the heart of the inner passage and is surrounded by glaciers, rainforest, and mountains. The Zimovia is the main road that runs about 14 miles along the west side of the island. There are a few paved roads in town and the rest are unpaved. The town of Wrangnell has one main library and one medical centre. The medical centre has 8 beds for acute care and 14 beds for long-term care. The present population is approximately 2,400 inhabitants. Photo taken in 2014.

Bahia Lapataia, or Lapatia Bay, is a desolate 240-square-mile expanse that at one time was home to the inhabitants of Tierra del Fuego. National Route 3 ends at Bahia Lapataia. This fjord, located at the far south end of Argentina, connects to the Beagle Channel and was originally carved out by the glaciers' movement. Photo taken in 2016.

Antarctica is the Southernmost continent. It contains about 90% of the world's ice and 70% of its fresh water. The continent spreads approximately 5,400,000 square miles. It has the coldest and driest climate on Earth. In July of 2010, the temperature hit a record low of -93 degree Celsius. In most areas, the snow never melts. Eventually, the snow compresses and becomes the glacier ice that makes up the ice sheet. Antarctica has few permanent residents. It has research stations and field camps that are staffed year-round. McMurdo station is the largest station with a population of one thousand people in the summer and two hundred in the winter.

Ushuaia is located in a wide bay on the southern most part of South America in the Terra del Fuego archipelago. It is nicknamed "End of the World." Ushuaia was named by the Yamanas Indians. It means "deep bay looking westward." Presently, most of the inhabitants come from northern Argentina. Photo taken in 2016

Jardin de roses, (La Roseraie) in Buenos Aires, Argentina. This beauty was created in 1924 by a landscaper named Carlos Thays. Here you can enjoy the fragrances of 12,000 rose bushes of many different colours. The garden makes available benches and water fountains for visitors' relaxation pleasure. La Roseraie is a real taste of legendary culture. Photo taken in 2016.

Himeji Castle is a world cultural heritage site also known as "White Castle." The castle was built about 400 years ago and stands as one of the largest and oldest castles. It has 21 gates that retain the styles of the Azuchi-Momoyam period (1574-1600). The castle was designed and built with 997 openings in the walls from which arrows and guns were shot. These openings are called *samas*. Photo taken in 2017.

Five storied Pagoda in Nikko, Japan. This Pagoda stands 35m high and has 5 tiers. From bottom to top the tiers represent: (1) Earth – our birth, (2) Water – adaptability to change, (3) Fire – motivation and strength, (4) Wind – freedom and development, (5) Sky – Buddhist thought or rebirth. The mountain town of Nikko is home to the Tosho-gu Shrine built by Tokugawa Iemitsu as a dedication to his grandfather, Shogun Tokugawa. Photo taken in 2017.

According to a variety of available studies, the healthiest people are the retirees who live in Sardinia, Italy. They routinely make time to walk approximately three to five miles a day preferably over the hillsides (Sardinia is mostly hillside) then return home for a social, espresso-coffee break. Sardinia is a place where retirees can benefit from the splendor of a coastal life style along the Mediterranean, enjoy beautiful beaches, take in the stunning natural beauty of the landscape, appreciate the exquisite presence of medieval castles and, most of all, revel in the affordable local cost of living. Sardinia is also known to have hot and dry summers, very little rain, and plenty of ventilation delivered by the sea breeze. There is a steady presence of sunshine hours throughout the year and good medical care is readily available and affordable. This is a place where men and women live almost the same length of time as centenarians. By all accounts, this place should be called the intersection of sophistication and longevity for the mature adults. *That's the life!*

I was surprised to learn there are also a number of designated places in the Philippines to which between thirty to forty thousand foreigners immigrate due to the relatively warm climate, reasonably low cost of living, and where medical practices are offered by U.S. trained doctors. Here, one can qualify for a permanent retiree visa when you are at least fifty years of age and earning over one thousand dollars a month in pension benefits.

Malaysia is another country where English is spoken fluently, there exists a good health-care system, warm climate, plenty of beautiful beaches, and a low crime rate. The present ten-year visa can easily be renewed and retirees can live a good life for approximately fifteen hundred to two thousand dollars a month.

Let's not forget about Spain and its cookery and cultural enchantments. Spain offers superb lavishness at an unassuming cost. The nation is ranked among the top ten for best places to retire because of its affordability and quality of life as long as you have approximately two hundred and fifty thousand dollars in savings to start out with.

However, to retire abroad and experience the life of a millionaire for a whole lot less money is a big decision. You must look at a number of factors and undertake extensive research about the intended destination prior to putting the consideration on the table. Of course, it helps if you have a sense of adventure, suffer from little or no medical frailties, are keen on exploring new retirement avenues, and money is not much of an issue. It's an effective principle for those daring senior citizens who choose this path to feel as though giving them a taste of what it might be like to live as a person of wealth. They are happy to accomplish all this without having to be reminded they don't possess the luxury to freely reach into a swollen wallet. They are equally unfazed by the fact they do not own huge stock options that can perform unabashed leaps and bounds to bring them gigantic returns. Their joy of living each new day to the fullest is more important than any happiness money could possibly buy them. I don't suspect these retirees envy the working class at all. This must hold particularly true when they sit back and watch the younger generation scurry through the early daylight hours for a chance at using the treadmill before they leave for work. Another noticeable trend is the struggle the younger people face as they try to garner a little motivation to slot in after-hour weight- lifting exercises, go jogging, or attend a yoga session after a long day on the job.

Figuring out how best to weigh the pros and cons of choosing between my present quick-paced business responsibilities and the liberty of a much slower stride is no longer an open question for me. Even if this melancholic situation is not meant to be my punitive direction-finding arrow that points to my "senior" status, I really am ready for my new freedom and time flexibility. In private, I keep revisiting the typical definition of a senior citizen as opposed to its full definition. Without question, the typical definition jumps out as a reference to a person aged sixty or more, although, it's not uncommon to hear people refer to them as "old persons." The full definition of a "senior" speaks primarily of a person who has retired. Quite frankly, I don't like either one of them. In my search for a more appealing definition, I learned that the Greek philosopher, Aristotle, thought of the seniors as "miserable beings who were out to satisfy their own selfish needs." In the context of the times, Aristole speaks of older citizens living by memory rather than by hope and "…are small minded because they have been humbled by life." They feel… "only contempt for other people's opinion of them." This is in keeping with the idea of their feeling devalued, which in many ways, I believe it stands as a justifiable concern.

It may ring true that most people commonly group together the portrayal of a senior, a retiree, a pensioner or an elderly with the same universal philosophy. Is all this hype a wholesale of short-sightedness about an age review of someone who is sixty-two to sixty-five years of age? Does this reference encompass those who have retired from their employment, receive pensions, passed middle age, and are looking for a little respect? Irrelevant of how we choose to refer to the ageing generation, we all have one thing in common; the pulse rate still reads sixty to one hundred beats per minute. That makes all of us "living mortals" with a trail of life experiences ready to share with anyone who wishes to pay attention and learn from them.

One day, if we're lucky, we'll all be steps away from retirement so why be apprehensive to take part in unreserved conversations with today's retirees or with the elderly? It's possible their experiences, whatever they might have been, could offer insights that may very well be the difference-makers of our daily lives.

I have high regards for the words spoken by Michel Legrand, the famous French music composer who, coincidently, shares the same birthday as mine. He explains the benefit of listening and learning very well. "The more I live, the more I learn, the more I realize, the less I know." Benjamin Franklin also spoke about learning. "Tell me and I forget, teach me and I remember. Involve me and I learn." Winston Churchill's words are also worth remembering: "I am always ready to learn although I do not always like being taught." The mere reference to these wise sayings prompted me to announce that my time was right, and that I had created a clean-cut partial-exit plan that befits my life style.

I must say that planning is a genuine life lesson in motion. When we combine this pursuit with affirmative action, we're able to draft a graph meant to evolve into a suitable scheme en route to our happiness. The process may be fun for some people, while for others, it may be a bitter pill that is difficult to swallow. Fortunately, for most people, planning creates an ambiance of discipline and order. It is with creative thinking and with the assistance of a vivid imagination that we establish and reach our pre-determined goals. Those are the same goals that enrich us with the luxury of cashing-in our pre-buildup proceeds in the later part of our lives. By practicing critical financial thinking in our younger years, we stand a good chance of making our retirement years a haven that doesn't harbour regrets or false anxiety. Why then, resist a good thing? Why hesitate to create a plan with the potential to bring rationality, structure, creativity, and satisfaction all into one scenario?

Although planning cannot totally predict the solidity of our future days, it can offer a boost of confidence and effectiveness if we're faced with unanticipated turns of events. Why not, then, give it the green light to move ahead with a doable blueprint and stick with that plan? Perhaps it's because we like to say we're too busy to follow through with it at the time. But, if that's the case, life will happen and we'll be stuck at the planning stage without the benefit of figuring out our full existence. For those who are fond of this selection, it's worth noting that inaction puts good sense in jeopardy if we fall into an unwelcome or comatose existence. In that predicament, people run the risk of losing out on retirement recompense because their no-plan theory miscarried.

Could it be possible that we just don't like to admit we're getting old? Does anyone like getting old? It's tough to accept that as we get closer to retirement, we see ourselves moving away from the age of curiosity and lean toward the age of longing. It would not be unheard of for some mature adults to dismiss the planning theory as an exercise of wasteful premeditation instead of seeing it as their chance to explore the opportunities life has to offer.

As the end of the summer approaches, I'm pleased to finally get past my querulous "should I or shouldn't I?" retirement mode. I'm now ready and all wound-up for change, but, I first want to arrange a lengthy discussion with my business accountant.

Secondly, I'm looking forward to engaging in a serious discourse with my family members who would understand my dilemma between the love for the business and my need to move on to other aspects of my life. After all, life is not all about work or sticking it out on the job for as long as you live. At last, I'm ready and prepped to make sure I don't deliver a crumbling speech to either the accountant or my family. Whatever the outcome might be, I'll meet it with relief because I value and appreciated their gut-driven expert input. As it turned out, the accountant made judicious and well thought-out suggestions, and my family promptly seconded, with great reference, my motion for change. Being the business operator I've been for so many years, I'm all too familiar with the gains from an outcome that means the difference between the results achieved from a prearranged to-do list or the failure suffered by not following through with the list. Any significant plan should have option "A" and option "B." Each option ought to be addressed with eagerness and glitz for the simple reason that positivity has the potential to motivate us in the direction of progress.

And so, without further adieu, on September 21st, a new life story began for me. It had nothing to do with the need to deal with a health issue, the desire to take an extended leave of absence, or to follow an outstanding fetish. It was merely my call to get in touch with reality. As of recently, I had become more and more aware of how I had changed with each fleeting milestone. The compass pointing me to the new destination told me I was still missing something. I needed a detailed daily planner that emphasized and exemplified my new purpose. Also, I still had to prepare a fully written and carefully edited exit announcement. Furthermore, I had not given myself an opportunity to mull over a pre- emptive timetable for a flexible work schedule.

With each option providing a new view, I felt certain that the alternative to engage in working from home was not a viable option for me. What I did have however, was the desire to be a little more involved with projects of a different nature. I was looking for initiatives that went a little ways beyond the scope of my present work both inside and outside of the office. While I trudged through many decision-making challenges in the past and managed to come out with only minor scratches and bruises most of the time, I'm older now and my forbearance level is not as high as it once was. So it was all coming down to timing and shrewd alternatives. I didn't think it wise to delay the inevitable much longer, especially when I was confident I could handle my life's changes in fairly large doses. I own up to the reality that just as over-thinking a situation can cause spells of confusion, wondering about it can promote puzzlement that seldom leads the way to specific destinations. I think the belief that life takes us wherever it wants us to go, and we're just going along for the ride, is all but an untamed myth. If we follow the confused passageway, we not only become our own obstacle, we open ourselves to the danger of blindly chasing anything that may represent falsehood. It's never too late to make changes or to accept that it's we who are changing. We are the living parties who should be thrilled and willing to celebrate each day and every change as it occurs.

Although I was familiar with such excellent sounding theories, I still wondered if this entire ruckus was actually adding up to inertia. I wanted to make a change, but at the same time, I didn't want to risk the security of what I knew and the protection of what I had. Was all this collective start-up mystery stacking up against me? Not likely. I vowed not to let myself get trapped in retirement analysis or revisit my decision every other week. Within a few short days, I prepared myself emotionally and physically to step up my progression toward a different and more buoyant world. My plan was to take a closer look at what appealed most to me, then move to close off the unlikely possibilities I had left unlocked in my repertoire far too long. It felt difficult at first, but then it came to me that the authenticity of my transitional plan must be no less than a qualified agent of change. It had to be original in nature, innovative, inclusive and with no foregone conclusion. The frankness of my expectations would not be sheltered by a one-size-fits all curriculum.

Being ready and pumped with renewed energy, I was now excited to introduce change in my life and my career.

Surprisingly, this newly generated synergy did not make me feel like I was becoming spellbound on a desolate roadway. Yes, I'm entering retirement, but I want to remain the person I've always been, although the outside world might see me as someone I'm not. All I'm hoping for is to make a constructive impact on issues that mattered most to me. Even a small bang arising from the fact that I'm alive and well and actively taking baby steps toward refashioning life's ways brings me gratification. By coincidence, my novel philosophy makes it natural for me to consider the following opportunity: write another non-fiction book, and once again donate the proceeds to the foundation of my choice.

Overall, I believe I have overcome my fear of ageing and the unknown. I have no doubt I'm making progress in favour of a new and different lifestyle that connects me to the people who share my strategy and the anguish of leaving the business behind. Another pillar of my self-made mandate is for me to put into place a successful adaptation statement. To ensure the anticipated impact, I needed to come up with a few creative tricks and draft a workable daily timetable. It was essential, or even obligatory, for me to be blunt about making key decisions that were relevant to *my* vision. The winning choice must be the antidote that cures any left-over woes I may previously have failed to take into account due to my demanding schedule. I have high hopes that this refinement of activities will be deserving of some personal fascination.

Given the choice, I prefer to tiptoe into this novel Infrastructure to push myself on and take serious notice of the world's shakiest quagmires. There are lots of lessons to be learned in order to gain even a modest bit of knowledge about the substantive practices of the world. Learning as we mature reminds me of a staircase: If you want to climb to the top, you must keep pushing on until you get there. But, if you let premeditated defeat label the objective "a terrible idea," you're likely to abandon the climb altogether and go back to where you started from. Retreating from a climb would hardly qualify as a preferred alternative because it feels too much like giving up. By selecting to go back to the bottom of the stairs, it means one didn't really want to reach the glow at the top of the staircase after all.

The following day, in a sweeping note scribbled in haste to myself, I wrote: "I don't get it; the selection to remain at the base of the stairs is economically inefficient and denies a person the opportunity to reach their potential. This has never been, nor will it ever become, an option for me. Not if I can help it." This is the note I refer to when I encounter gloomy days.

It feels like a striking flash to learn how the carte du jour for taking calculated chances and embracing feasible possibilities played out for me. Knowing what I know today, I think we all play a part in our own destiny. In that spirit, I suggest we do our financial homework through our younger years then go after screened retirement opinions during our mature existence. This can be accomplished without letting our emotions boil over or by bringing prejudice into the picture. The legitimacy of my willingness to change, coupled with the desire to get the most out of a duly planned exit strategy has now come into full swing. My full-time work responsibilities will soon be trimmed down to part- time and, anecdotally speaking, I hear myself say: "I'm really growing some interest in this transition." At one point, I had to stop for a brief second just to recollect and refresh my thoughts because the words I heard coming out of my mouth differed extensively from those I had instinctively spoken dozens of times before. The present words sounded thin-skinned and artificial even to me. Fundamentally, my excitement for the upcoming change was steadily growing.

There is no need for me to daydream about the way to predict how my new free time will lead the way to write another true-life book. In the last four years, I squeezed-out and made use of each free minute of each day to write and publish two non-fiction books. The process took discipline and a lot of learning, but I don't regret one second of the time I used to bring each project to fruition. Once I published the first book, I realized that writing is another way of talking to an audience who is willing to hear what I have to say. Writing gives me purpose. Writing allows me to savor the preparation time and incites me to sharpen my drafting techniques. To write a good quality story requires never-ending editing, it forces the writer to think, and it encourages a sharing of sentiments. I definitely find writing to be a stress-relieving exercise with the end result promising to grant energizing public reactions. My subjects are real and I take great delight in sharing my business entrepreneurship experiences hoping they will benefit new entrants. But one success story does not necessarily constitute emancipation for all concerned.

SLOWING DOWN

It was quite a sobering experience to begin the partial winding down from my long running business environment. In an effort to lessen the woes and flip this situation into a positive twist, I authenticated my desire to fine-tune the slowing down procedure. As I started to get my bearings in gear, my eyes slowly betrayed me and involuntarily began to water. This time, I held my head high, knowing my resolution was correct. My time for a retirement move was right and it was now! Without further dithering, I arranged to meet with my financial consultant one more time. This time, the encounter would serve the purpose of finalizing and signing off on a well-tailored business downsizing arrangement. Although this type of discussion had been circling around via emails and several telephone conversations, on this face-to-face occasion, the deal was sealed without regret.

My decision was met with great support and enthusiasm from family and friends. However, not many of them believed I would actually follow through with the new modus vivendi (life style). Yet it wasn't until after the semi-retirement announcement that I opened a new dialogue and proudly shed the manacles that had kept me tied to the business sphere for over twenty-seven years.

I'm being honest almost to a fault when I say I'm a little on edge to begin blocking the intended subject of discussion for my third book. But then my spirit lit up as soon as I told myself to drop the doubts and make good on the greater objective - donate the proceeds from the book to lend a helping hand to the weakened and the unfortunate citizens of the world. I'm referring to the women and children who, through no fault of their own, are robbed of their guiltless character and forced to become the receivers and sufferers of the most appalling offenses. Not a good situation for the injured parties of war-torn countries, authoritarian regime-controlled nations, and poverty stricken areas. There seems to be a shortage of sobriety in the world. Basic human needs and personal safety should be supported everywhere.

For a few years now, I have steadily developed an unremitting desire to help those who work hard to bring hope to the most unprotected circles of our society. I frequently make this reference to the children who live in grave conditions and to the children whose health care is non-existent. Each day they struggle against extreme poverty. Their water supplies are severely limited and personal safety is unheard of. The dental hygiene we have access to and which some of us even take for granted, is highly controversial and of great concern in some countries. We all deserve a chance to look at our life as a precious souvenir. All of us should have the opportunity to live our days to the fullest potential. It would be considered less harmonious of us not to act upon whatever constructive action we can champion in order to extend a helping hand to the less fortunate. My message comes from the heart and is much bigger than a few nice words spoken at random or on impulse. The essence of my appeal is to apply pressure against such sub-human conditions because those unfortunate beings deserve better. Is it so hard to be realists? It's of immeasurable worth to help the disadvantaged believe their unspeakable living conditions will be corrected one day. When that day comes, these victims will get back on their feet and claim victory in the face of the villains who, by imposing unorthodox acts, have robbed them of their basic human dignity. They will gather the courage to stand up to cruelty and abuse and shout "No more!" This will be their moment to shine and tell the world that through hope, a helping hand, and loud voices, anything can be made possible. They may be the last people to believe in this actuality, but at minimum, our efforts and determination will fend off some of their despair.

I have no axe to grind, only a mission to be accomplished. I am referring to a mission that doesn't speak in quiet tones but rather, sounds more like an ear-splitting horn. The message is clear and the demand is non-negotiable: abuse against the less prosperous and, women and children must stop! It's time the ghastly characters, villains, or whatever else we wish to identify them as, find a different planet to live on because the civilized people of Earth will, in effect, punish them for their brutal actions. I'm not prepared to watch a humanitarian mission end without an encouraging conclusion. Most of all, I'm not an ally of disappointment where children's livelihood and safety is concerned. I'm definitely not willing to approach this issue by looking for easy pacifications. The more I learn about such gross injustices and prejudices, the less I understand the debacle. These conditions speak the harsh truths about the inconceivably callous abuse that has been allowed to confiscate our civilized footing throughout the world. Most striking for me is the lack of awe-inspiring government-issued directives.

Growing up, I thought the government was the people's hero. In my mind, a hero was a person or a governing body with the talent and courage to save the day. Now that I'm older and more experienced, I think the jury has been out on this deliberation for a long time. To my point, the federal vehicle carrying the overdue sponsorship to support not-for-profit agencies trample all over this preposterous misery is driving on flat tires. The worst part is, the vehicle has no inflator kit available to ensure it gets to the intended destination in a timely fashion. I have so many questions, but there are so few reasonable answers available.

We must remember that after the Second World War, The United Nations General Assembly drafted an International Bill of Rights to ensure such atrocities never happened again. The United Nations representatives were intellectuals who came from different cultural, religious, and political backgrounds. The Declaration put into plain site the idea that all human beings are equal. It promoted respect for the rights and freedoms of all individuals, re-affirmed their faith in dignity, addressed the worth of a human being, and equal right for men and women. Although we don't see the word children mentioned in the text, it is understood that children's rights were based on human rights. With the passing of years, the suggestion that our civilized world is keeping those good intentions alive is looking anemic. However perplexing the disregard for human rights is today, we must bear in mind that at the time of inception, the United Nations voiced its doubts about a successful outcome for the proposed equality concept. So far, they have been untiringly chipping away at those doubts each day and at any rally possible since 1948. They keep pushing ahead by doing their most diligent work and by making a firm statement that they will not give up until they accomplish the equality objective. They have faced-off with many delay tactics and obstructions in many areas of the world, especially where it's still believed that women and children are nothing more than disposable commodities. Even if the UN approached this mission in large numbers and with tight fists, it will take many more years to effectively dismantle those operatives. The perpetrators have been able to flourish without accountability for too long. Those malefactors use the unprotected circles of society to produce financial substance and personal gratification, especially when they offer a six-or-nine year old girl to a warrior in recognition of a job well done.

I don't think I'm alone when I say there is a good chance these sick characters are not only laughing in defiance but they blatantly threaten to up their antes. What am I to make of this colossal wrongdoing? How can I, one person, possibly make any difference? As other waves of concerned citizens are already engaged in collecting the required evidence to fight the underworld operators and bring them to justice, it was rather disturbing to hear that the outlaws were hardly running scared. They deliberately and blatantly send reasoned messages to the leaders of private organizations, charities, and international rescue agencies, stating they don't need to ask for permission to keep doing what they do. Their enterprise does not need to be registered with any governmental ministry, nor are they expected to pay taxes for their inexorable earnings. They give wretchedness a different meaning. The heartbreaking sticky point here is that these ruthless brokers are so brain-washed and terrified of any backlash that they idolize only their leader and the almighty dollar. Such inexcusable human actions permanently affect and damage many families, individuals, children, adults, and institutional workers in the most critically negative ways. Is the care and respect for human kind a fallacy? Does social equality suffer from a lack of forethought?

It became clear that the main deliverable of my prospective plan was to highlight areas in which my expertise and commitment would provide the most benefits. I quickly recognized that the atrocities against the most vulnerable were so many and so gross, and the resources for help were so few and scattered. Medical professionals and other volunteers face burn-out day in and day out, but they don't give in to exhaustion. At times, fatigue acts like a shadow that follows volunteers around just waiting to pick them up when they drop from overtiredness. I readily confess that I detest vulnerability and I'm sure this revelation hardly comes as a surprise to anyone who knows me.

In further conversations about semi-retirement with my family and friends, it became evident I had found my fated niche. Not only did they agree with my choice, they clapped at my conviction. They admired my dedication for the cause and wished me much success. I knew this would not be an easy task to get ahead of. Along with a great number of other volunteers, I aspired to bring a spinning element to what I call "an evolution, for ALL people of the world."

Hiding my disappointment that such dramatic facts have been somewhat suppressed or purposely kept in the dark throughout the years, I developed an interest in the purpose and the work ethics of the RINJ Foundation (Rape Is No Joke.) Their mission is to follow the trail of evidence, collect available data and bring hardened criminals of the sex trade to justice. I'm committed to help young girls between the ages of six and nine who are abducted and mercilessly sold into the sex trade. Those voiceless victims are in desperate need of assistance. They face an immense struggle thinking of a counterattack to shake off the terror of their present circumstances let alone hope to stay alive. One day, the callous perpetrators will no longer celebrate a day at the expense of the less fortunate. One day, the children will get their long-awaited break granting them the power and fortitude to stand up and be counted. For now, it is the younger children who are most at risk and in need of physical and mental aid. They have become the executioners' preferred trade mark. In the eyes of those cruel brokers, the most innocent young beings are worth an extra dollar. The highest bidder can easily buy a six year old girl from Lebanon, Jordan, Iraq, or Syria for one hundred American dollars. They have no qualms about selling her off for the purpose of being raped, abused, and often times killed. It is extremely hard, if not impossible, to fathom how easily the trading transaction is done. This type of business deal is sealed without an iota of remorse or a bloody mark to stain their dark conscience. The blasphemy dished out to any abductees who dare to cry for help, or who refuse to cooperate, is appalling. Ruthless abductors think nothing of bringing out a large group of kidnapped girls and killing them right in front of the girl who is crying or screaming "No!!!!" The death of those girls is affixed directly to that little girl's mind. These unspeakable and horrific crimes need to be monitored closely and the offenders *must be prosecuted*. What could possibly be taking our civilized society so long to turn things around?

In the past two years, I used whatever tools were at my disposal to bring more awareness to the general public about these wide-spread dire conditions. So far, I have eluded negative debates and stumbling blocks that have the potential to negatively impact my efforts to push forward with subject awareness and watchfulness. From my perspective, awareness is evenly matched to knowledge. Knowledge holds the power to define human perils. It has the capacity to organize and secure both the institutional and political leverage necessary to stamp out the brutal atrocities liberally inflicted on the children of the world. Knowledge holds the key to the locked gate that is oftentimes rendered invisible to too many people for too many years. Knowledge has the strength and the ability to wipe out harmful conundrums and open the flood gates of accountability, respect, order, and change. Knowledge contains the last word when it comes to eradicating the malevolence that has been permitted to battle against civilization for so long.

I have my own select views as to why the face of despair has forever been jostled and tolerated throughout the world. This is the main reason that spiked my interest in supporting the affirmative actions practiced by the RINJ Foundation. This federally registered Canadian foundation is committed to provide whatever medical aid, psychological counseling, food, clothing, and shelter they can secure for the neediest. The volunteer medical team often finds it necessary to perform reconstructive surgery to minimize the young girls' facial damage ruthlessly carried out by abductors. As a result of defacing the prisoner or slave, the captors put on display their unquestionable power. The foundation's hard work inevitably tries to create a noteworthy imprint in the memory of survivors that rises above the torment they suffered. Understandably, any hope or optimism will hang about as the winning strategy for another day.

In most, if not all cases, the injured party's progress toward healing is a seriously difficult undertaking. It must match or be greater than their infinite will to distance themselves from the past tyrannically imposed outrage they endured. Through the RINJ Foundation, these wounded victims are nurtured and encouraged to transform their misfortune into a worthy day-to-day living exercise. The convincing point for being a participant of this foundation emerged the day I began reading more and more articles about the work done by this organization and the challenges taken head-on by these determined individuals. Even when the stories were told in their simplest form, and by means of reference to so much critical evidence, the agency's consistent and rock-solid work spoke of heroism. Tendering assistance and building hope for the unfortunate has been the foundation's unchanged currency for many years. I joined as a member of the RINJ Foundation and was later elected as one of the agency's active board members.

I did not need an invitation to begin my task with the aim to transform the community's outlook from "I cannot do anything about this dire situation" to "where do I sign up to help?" I was elated to unilaterally undertake to run used clothing and toy collections to benefit those in desperate need of consolation. I also busied myself with sourcing appropriate agencies with the infrastructure to supply large quantities of medicinal aid and vaccines for the purpose of shipping fifty-pound kits to the medical staff working with the distressed and most vulnerable - underprivileged children. With sadness permeating on my face, I accepted that to push this worthwhile cause to the nation's forefront required concrete and open-ended commitment. But how much commitment would be sufficient? I didn't want to know the answer to that question.

Sitting in the quietude of my house, the solid silence was more felt than heard. I dropped my sweater on a chair and sat down in deep thought. How do we try to justify the fact that, we sometimes, make a big deal out a triviality? I felt a headache coming on, rationalizing what those unfortunate human beings think of a daily triviality. I'd bet they consider it as having a great day. There are no delusions about the severity of the soul-devastating practices in the sex slave industry. So far, I haven't crossed paths with panic or hysteria as I stay in the loop of the foundation's arduous push to move forward without trepidation when coming to the aid of defenseless human beings. Advocating for full accountability of the heartless madmen who commit such deplorable crimes is the respectable thing to do.

That afternoon, I had to take a long and deep breath just to relax my jaw before I was ready to carry on objectively. The foundation's motto that the search for the guilty and the punishment for their crimes must be adequately resourced and high-quality rules must prevail is the logical approach. Awareness of the facts will not permit these benevolent efforts to lay abandoned on the desk of some person of authority. I would argue that by speaking out as a group, our voices and requests for the long overdue protection of the most susceptible will undoubtedly be heard and the message ultimately understood. Our message should be delivered with a note and a tone that simply says: "This demand is not open to discussion."

Confirmation of my new mission's positioning received to some extent, an almost hysterical reaction from some of the people who know me. These days, there is no shortage of sardonic chitchat floating around about my delegation of energy to an adopted organization. Many acquaintances have remarked that if I had wanted to keep going at such serious pace I shouldn't have cut the umbilical cord from my business. Then there are those who do not have such a narrow-minded view and are quick to extend their congratulations to me for choosing a well-balanced mixture of part-time work and being a part-time affiliate of a not-for- profit foundation. I also have talks with people who are essentially impartial to my actions. In the nature of things, all these external diverging opinions do not and will not have any negative implications on my new objective. There is no question I'm happy with my decision to be among hundreds of other concerned citizens and volunteers who vigorously work toward the call to break ground and set the world's focus in a new direction. I'd like to believe that the window of opportunity for probing into wrongdoings against humanity is embarking on a radical course of action. In real meaning, the reference to my semi- retirement status may bear some consideration as to whether I'm choosing it for the purpose of getting a little rest and relaxation or, for satisfying my golden rule to summon attention to the abnormal temperaments of life that subsists around us.

Whatever my true reason, I'm going into this adventure with my eyes wide open. I know full well that the adventure I'm embarking on could prove to be both a bit risky and a bit rewarding. It goes without saying that I don't want to focus on the hazards or the "what ifs" of the situation. Instead, I'm primed and utterly prepared to accept either crap or, *'nice one'* as the events unfolded. After all, I know I'm on the hook to get to my intended destination.

Once I cleared my slate of all the uncertainties about what to do with my free time in the upcoming retirement days, I conceded that my pre-planned endeavors may not all fit in my to-do list. I'm touched by a slight concern that it may be difficult to accommodate the extra travelling I've been postponing for years due to my significant work responsibilities. Travelling, for me, is a blueprint of multiple streams of interactions. I always get excited looking for new destinations and new cultures. I enjoy the planning process that includes making cost-efficient determinations, proper reservations, cashing in travel points, organizing what to pack, and looking into any possible contingency notifications. But there's one thing I'm a lot less enthusiastic about - the obligation to check for travel alerts which might ultimately jeopardize my plans. Arriving at this pivotal point of my life had been a long time coming. No more knots of dismay churned in my stomach. I'm almost ready for this inevitable life changer.

Before gearing up into semi-retirement mode, I decided to take a short break from work to test my endurance once away from daily business activities. For the first week, I spent my time at home lounging around in comfortable attire and doing not much more than checking my emails and text messages. As anticipated, that type of low-level activity didn't exactly pan out to my liking. In order to spur thing up, I turned my attention to the television set for a chance to catch some interesting political breaking news. As luck would have it, Mr. Chaotic, the nation's leader presiding not far from the Canadian border, has a habit of making sure he supplies the general public with plenty of questionable behavior. It hasn't take him long to earn the title of a political buffoon. Most of his high judicial opinions seem to lack expertise and most certainly don't help his rating positioning. To me, he doesn't come across as an emissary of professional material either on home turf or anywhere else. His low-end actions coupled with his poor attitude speak of unethical political goings on within his domain. After a while, that option didn't add much joviality or stimulation to my days.

By the time the second week rolled around, I had developed a somber demeanor and had not made much progress toward an adjustment to a lesser action-based day. My separation from work proved to be much harder than I had expected. I soon began missing the incessant incoming phone calls, the sound of the paging system announcing who the call was for, the business service hype, the frequent funny and facetious comments from staff and field operators, the lively sign language, and the less-than-colorful verbiage used in a quick reply to a ridiculous operation question. To some people, this racket might sound like a recipe for commotion, but to me, it represented a business sphere with impact, influence and longevity. My lifelong experience contends that vision plus calculated actions produce results. I live to see results. Quite often, the presence of constructive situational outcomes awakes personal contentment, and it generates positive aura throughout the office. Yes, the time of rest felt good, and the stillness was an added bonus for a day or two, but then an empty expanse began creeping in and invaded my space. Personal anxiety asserted itself at the same time as a void loomed ahead, alleging that business was running fine without me. Oh no! I'm replaceable? *Such deliberation really sucks.*

Business is and has always been my heartfelt nucleus. How was it possible that my absence was not missed all that much? The presumed feel-good factor that for most people is gained when they take a short leave from work, for me, turned out to be a total misnomer. My sense of purpose only recovered and soared again when I returned to my work station. On that day, my head actually stopped hurting, and the confused emotions, which, in the last week had caused me to roll my eyes, were blown away.

The very next day, I aligned my semi-retirement underlying principle with my promise to make good on some serious travels. I also added a hint of desire to starting my third writing project and doing a little volunteer work in the days to come. I carefully drafted a reasonable window of time for my new directive, ensuring the undertakings did not spill out all over the calendar.

Travelling for me is a carry-over from the geography course that in my much earlier school years scored only a second-rate mark. The fact that I didn't excel in that program can be attributed to the TITB (teacher is to blame) philosophy. That feeble explanation was a cover up for any student's inability or unwillingness to pay attention in class. Asking the teacher questions in order to alleviate the confusion brought on by a misunderstood lesson was not a cool thing to do in those days. Making the extra effort to try harder and collaborate with school authorities was also not a directive listed on some students' wish list. I happened to be one of those students who insisted on working with a very short geography assignment list. Memories….heck, they're humbling. Thinking back to things I said and did in my teens and early twenties, I remember people calling me a difficult individual. When I reached my forties and fifties, if I said anything that wasn't to usual standards, I was considered a person with a strange attitude. But now that I'm in my sixties, if I do or say similar things, I'm told I'm losing it.

As a mature person, the excuses that encircled me in yesteryears have assumed a different meaning. As an adult, I've become a believer that learning and adjusting to change are two things that remain constant in our lives. Perhaps one can say that my fondness for these words is a little presumptive. When my time came to make a life-altering change and learn to adapt to a slower paced life style, I suddenly struggled with doubts, gloomy moods, and plenty of resistance. But throughout my ambiguity, I remained unwavering in staying the course and honouring the commitment to walk my talk. In the process, new ideas and more openings for atonement descended like hailstones until the day my mind and soul merged to elicit not only a resolution, but a fitting panacea.

Now, a full year has passed since I began coasting toward slowing down. It had taken a while for me to get excited about the prospect of retirement or semi-retirement, and to get motivated enough to devise a different goal for the years ahead. The process has required a lot of thinking along with a certain behavioral attitude to move through the most important steps for chronicling the preferred outcome. It has been tricky and complicated to picture retirement when I've lived a life driven by productivity, measuring and managing my own companies' financial preparedness, understanding economic shifts, and addressing various business trade-offs. Today, I'm happy to cash-in on the consolation that no one has ever suggested I get out of my office, have a good look around, call a cab, get to the airport, buy a one way ticket, board a plane, and go somewhere far away from my comfort zone.

THE GROUNDWORK DAYS

Twenty-three thousand six hundred fifty-two days and counting is where I am on this sun-shining day of the fall season. The outside looks glamorous and peaceful. Autumn leaves are dropping from the trees with perfect precision, while indoors, standing as if at attention by the refrigerator, I'm silently calculating the real substance of a human being. In my anticipation to come up with the most correct answer, I had to be sure not to underestimate my evaluations or find room for ill-will. In the end, I concluded that life is an open door to passionate education. It encompasses every element and stage of our lives, beginning with personal care all the way to communication strategy, personal habits, learning skills, investment strategies, social interaction, financial tactics, work ethics, business acumen, and political wisdom. However, if we attempt to over-hunt for success whether it is for riches or status, we could land in ruin. When that happens, we try to put all blame on correctness instead of the real culprit - forgetting that for the most part, we are the real actors of our own screen play.

The next day, I arose at first light with the prime intend of turning those moralities into reality. I observed how fast the day was running by without waiting for people to adjust their moods. Before the next morning dawned, I concluded that at my age, my recently formulated exit plan was rightfully paving the way to a less stressful place. And with that conciliatory thought, I was, in fact, looking forward to my new life and new surroundings.

Blitzing through mixed thoughts with the intention to reflect and assess where my life's passage had taken me, I wondered whether in most cases my decisions for sensible survival of both my personal and business existences had been selected and executed with inspiring objectivity. Today, I'm no longer the little girl with ponytails. I'm no longer playing the busy bee who rushed through life taking a shot at making use of every minute of her waking hours. Today, I simply wonder if the intensity of each of my previous experiences might be enough to fashion the experience necessary to simplify my life's journey in the days to come.

I readily confess that the passing of years has undoubtedly taught me perspective. In effect, it's this viewpoint that brought to light the realization that life can make tough demands on us. Sometimes, life approaches us with what could be classified as a cynical heart and regularly leaves us with disappointing and frustrating results. But life goes on and so must we.

Back in the childhood formative years, I speculated what my future might look like through a grey lens, but - now that I'm sixty plus, I look back at those days with a more judicious understanding, a sense of clarity, and with true meaning. By the time I reached the present juncture, my evolving experiences have already discounted my childhood naivety, and rallied to make candid references to the base of my foundation. To a large extent, we stand to gain benefits from getting a grip on our past. It's vital to be apprised of our surroundings and to know that we don't have to go the distance alone. There is always hindsight to help us examine the past and re-assess it with the light of current awareness. I now look at the past as a valuable asset for the present because it has the potential to give me the strength to delve into the unknown to visualize the future and my aspirations. I am particularly attentive to living this stage of my life in the present tense and not letting the future slip back to photocopy the past.

In conclusion, having a foundation in our younger years definitely increases our chances at success for the present and minimizes the trepidation of what is still to come. Not recognizing or caring about the good and the not-so-good deeds of the days gone by may indeed be deserving of a slap on our wrist, and I, similar to what many other mature adults often do, asked myself whether I should have known better or done things differently. Without any unnecessary dithering, I have this response: "I am now old enough to know that I did the best I could with what I had to work with." With that genuine confirmation, I know I've grasped the full meaning of my existence. I totally accept this awe-inspiring transitory character of age, and I call it a wonderful gift. As for the rest, let the rain drops fall where they may. The sun is sure to come up again another day.

My compliments to you for taking the time to read my book.

I hope my narrative brought to light the gleaming emotions that oftentimes overtake our sense of being and of purpose as we approach the mature adult phase of our lives.

I could not have written this book with such personal depth of feelings about relinquishing the reins of a business before I experienced the separation from my own business in favour of retirement.

Whether your familiarity with the departure from work is similar to mine or far away from my reality, I know the memories of our time will be with us for the rest of our days.

Best wishes

Rose Catalano

ABOUT THE AUTHOR

Rose Catalano is the CEO of two security service companies. She is also the author of This Head of Security Wears High Heels and A Child's Voyage to New Life. Rose currently lives in Vaughan, Ontario, Canada.

www.ingramcontent.com/pod-product-compliance
Lightning Source LLC
Chambersburg PA
CBHW071413070526
44578CB00003B/570